NEW VANGUARD 318

TANKS IN OPERATION
BAGRATION 1944

The demolition of Army Group Center

STEVEN J. ZALOGA   ILLUSTRATED BY FELIPE RODRÍGUEZ

OSPREY PUBLISHING

Bloomsbury Publishing Plc

Kemp House, Chawley Park, Cumnor Hill, Oxford OX2 9PH, UK

29 Earlsfort Terrace, Dublin 2, Ireland

1385 Broadway, 5th Floor, New York, NY 10018, USA

E-mail: info@ospreypublishing.com

www.ospreypublishing.com

OSPREY is a trademark of Osprey Publishing Ltd

First published in Great Britain in 2023

A catalog record for this book is available from the British Library.

ISBN: PB 9781472853950; eBook: 9781472853929; ePDF 9781472853943; XML: 9781472853936

23 24 25 26 10 9 8 7 6 5 4 3 2 1

Index by Alan Rutter
Typeset by PDQ Digital Media Solutions, Bungay, UK
Printed and bound in India by Replika Press Private Ltd.

AUTHOR'S NOTE

Unless otherwise noted, the photos here are from the author's collection.

GLOSSARY

Abteilung	German battalion
AFV	Armored Fighting Vehicle
FH	*Feldherrnhalle*: honorific title of some *Heer* units
Front	Soviet equivalent of *Heeresgruppe* or Army Group
GD	*Grossdeutschland* (Greater Germany) unit designation
Heer	Army
Heeresgruppe	Army Group, a German formation of several armies
HG	*Heeresgruppe*: Army group, formation of several corps
HVAP	High-Velocity, Armor Piercing (Projectile)
KStN	*Kriegsstärkenachweisungen*: War establishment strength
OKH	*Oberkommando des Heeres:* Army High Command
Panzerjäger (Pz.Jg.)	Tank destroyer
s.Pz.Abt.	*schwere Panzer-Abteilung*: Heavy tank battalion
s.Pz.Jg.Abt.	*schwere Panzerjäger-Abteilung:* Heavy tank destroyer battalion
Sturmgeschütz	Assault gun
SU	*Samokhodnaya ustanovka*: self-propelled weapon
Tonnes	Metric ton (1,000kg; 2,200lbs)
Wehrmacht	(German) armed forces

CONTENTS

TANKS IN OPERATION *BAGRATION* 1944

The demolition of Army Group Center

INTRODUCTION

The tank battles on the Russian Front in the summer of 1944 pitted a growing Soviet tank force against an increasingly beleaguered Panzer force. This book surveys the principal tank types on both sides, as well as tank surrogates such as the tank destroyer/*Panzerjäger*, and the assault gun/*Sturmgeschütz*. Due to space limitations, it does not cover self-propelled field artillery or light armored vehicles such as armored cars and half-tracks. For convenience's sake, the term "AFV" (Armored Fighting Vehicle) in this book refers to the tank surrogates such as assault guns and tank destroyers.

DOCTRINE AND ORGANIZATION

Wehrmacht

Due to the heavy drain of Panzer divisions to the West in the spring of 1944, the Wehrmacht on the Russian Front had a significant imbalance in its Panzer units with assault guns and tank destroyers outnumbering the Panzers. Unlike the Red Army, Panzers were assigned to the Panzer divisions with the main exception being several Tiger battalions. As a result, there were no Panzer units specifically for infantry support. Instead, Sturmgeschütz units were used for infantry support instead of the tank units found in most other major armies.

Tank and AFV types: West vs East, summer 1944 (as percentages)			
	Panzer	StuG	Panzerjäger
West	69.0	20.2	10.7
East	44.5	39.8	15.6

The fighting on the right bank of the Dniepr in early 1944 had crippled a number of Panzer divisions and substantially reduced the strength of most others. By the early summer of 1944, there were 15 Panzer divisions, seven Panzergrenadier divisions, and six Tiger battalions on the Russian Front. These units were significantly understrength compared to the official *Kriegsstärkenachweisungen* (KStN: War establishment strength). Six Panzer divisions were so badly decimated that they were recalled to Germany for complete rebuilding. This did not occur in a timely fashion due to shortages, but the 6. and 19.Panzer-Divisionen returned from Germany to the Russian Front after the start of Operation *Bagration* in spite of their incomplete state.

Shortfalls of tanks and AFV on the Russian Front			
Tank/AFV	Jun 1, 1944	Jul 1, 1944	Aug 1, 1944
PzKpfw IV	1,479	1,037	897
Panther	360	479	177
Tiger	6	43	47
StuG	0	114	446
Panzerjäger	976	589	440
Total	**2,821**	**2,262**	**2,007**

The intended composition of Panzer divisions in the summer of 1944 was a Panzer Regiment with a battalion of PzKpfw IV and a battalion of Panther tanks. Of the 15 Panzer divisions, only eight had their intended Panther battalion at the start of Operation *Bagration*. On paper, a German Panzer division had 170 tanks but on June 1, they averaged only about 60 tanks each or about a third of their authorized strength. In some cases, StuG III assault guns were deployed in lieu of tanks.

The majority of Waffen-SS Panzer divisions were deployed in the West in the summer of 1944 with only two, "Totenkopf" and "Wiking," serving on the Russian Front at the start of the summer campaign. The Fallschirm-Panzer-Division "Hermann Göring" was pulled out of Italy on July 12, 1944. It left its armored vehicles behind and was hastily re-equipped with 64 PzKpfw IV and 31 Jagdpanzer IV before being rushed to the Warsaw area in time for the August 1944 battles.

The Panzergrenadier divisions nominally contained a single Panzer-Abteilung, but these were generally equipped with StuG III assault guns due to the shortage of turreted tanks.

A PzKpfw IV Ausf G of 4.Panzerarmee passes through the burning ruins of the Ukrainian town of Zhitomir during the January 1944 fighting with the 1st Ukrainian Front.

Panzer units on the Russian Front June 1, 1944				
Unit	PzIV	Panther	Tiger	StuG
Heeresgruppe Nord				
12.Pz.Div.	35+14*			
s.Pz.Abt.502			33+24	
11.SS-Pz.Gr.Div. "Nordland"		5+7		
Heeresgruppe Mitte				
20.Pz.Div.	49+7			
25.Pz.Gr.Div.				41+7
Pz.Gr.Div.FHH	8+9			6+11
s.Pz.Abt.501			29+8	
Heeresgruppe Nord-Ukraine				
1.Pz.Div.	33+1	23+3		
4.Pz.Div.	68+2			
5.Pz.Div.	57+2			
7.Pz.Div.	34+13			
8.Pz.Div.	10+1	73+7		
16.Pz.Div.	43+5	4+6		12+7
5.SS-Pz.Div. "Wiking"	27	77+1		20+1
18.Pz.Gr.Div.				43+1
20.Pz.Gr.Div.				
s.Pz.Abt.505			36+6	
s.Pz.Abt.506			39+2	
s.Pz.Abt.507			45+2	
s.Pz.Abt.509			37+9	
Heeresgruppe Süd				
3.Pz.Div.	12+7			
13.Pz.Div.	2+1			
14.Pz.Div.	1+34			2+1
17.Pz.Div.	28+8			
23.Pz.Div.	10	26+26		
24.Pz.Div.	36+4			15+1
3.SS-Pz.Div."Totenkopf"	23+5		2+6	
10.Pz.Gr.Div.				9+1
Pz.Gr.Div. "Grossdeutschland"	8+6	30+25	12+8	
Sub-total	*484+119*	*238+75*	*233+65*	*148+30*
Total	**603**	**313**	**298**	**178**
*Operational + in repair				

In response to the unfolding disaster in Belarus, on July 2, 1944, Hitler proposed a mini-Panzer division based around a Panzergrenadier battalion with armored half-tracks and a Panzer-Gruppe with 30–40 Panzers plus supporting anti-tank and anti-aircraft guns. He indicated the need for at least 12 of these formations and suggested that they be designated as a brigade. The OKH (Army High Command) advocated using the cadres from Panzer divisions being rebuilt in Germany to form the basis for these units since Hitler wanted them to start entering service by mid-August. They also reconfigured the reserve Panzer divisions based in Germany for this program. These new formations sopped up a significant portion of newly manufactured tanks in the summer of 1944. For example, of the approximately 735 new Panthers delivered in July–August 1944, 335 (46%) went to the new Panzer brigades and only 340 to the Russian Front (46%).

A PzKpfw IV Ausf H waits alongside a Sd.Kfz.251/6 radio command half-track during the September 1944 fighting.

The first of these, Panzer-Brigade.101, was rushed to the Russian Front in mid-August 1944. It took part along with the improvised SS-Panzer-Brigade "Gross" in Operation *Doppelkopf* that aimed to restore contact between Heeresgruppe Nord and Heeresgruppe Mitte in late August 1944. Three more of these brigades (102, 103, 104) were also hastily sent into action in late August 1944 in the Baltic region with Heeresgruppe Nord. Their hasty organization and limited training resulted in disappointing combat performance. The next series of brigades were deployed to the West starting in September 1944.

The other major non-divisional Panzer formation was the heavy tank battalion (*schwere Panzer-Abteilung*), equipped with Tiger I tanks. There were six of these on the Russian Front at the start of Operation *Bagration*. This was one of the few categories of Panzer units where the Russian Front exceeded the Normandy deployments, with only two Tiger battalions in Normandy at the time. Most of these were concentrated in HG Nord-Ukraine. Compared to other Panzer units, the Tiger battalions were well-equipped and close to their KStN establishment.

Separate from the Panzer units were the army Sturmgeschütz brigades that were raised and trained by the artillery branch. Although called brigades, they were in fact of battalion size. There were two KStN in effect, the basic 1942 pattern with 31 per brigade (22 StuG with the 7.5cm gun and nine StuH with the 10.5cm howitzer) and an upgraded February 1944 table with 45 vehicles (33 StuG and 12 StuH). There was a significant shortage of assault guns, so only a handful of units had the February 1944 organization. In late 1943, plans were underway to upgrade the assault gun

Panzer Lehr Division was one of a number of Panzer units allotted to the Russian Front prior to the Normandy landings, only to be redirected to France after D-Day. This is a Panther Ausf A of Panzer-Lehr-Rgt.130 during deployment in Hungary in the spring of 1944.

units into a combined arms formation with added Grenadier and Panzer escort units (*Begleit-Batterie*). The infantry escort was intended to provide support for the assault guns against hostile infantry. The tank escort was equipped with obsolete PzKpfw II light tanks and was intended to provide firepower against enemy anti-tank guns and infantry. By July 1944, only three brigades were upgraded to this configuration and renamed as a Heeres-Sturmgeschütz-Artillerie-Brigade.

StuG brigades on the Russian Front, summer 1944				
	June	**July**	**August**	**September**
StuG brigades	32	32	31	28
StuG*	615 + 158	718 + 108	463 + 175	383 +173
StuH	95 + 25	123 + 16	116 + 32	135 + 57
Sub-total	710 + 215	841 + 156	579 + 238	518 + 258
Total	**925**	**997**	**817**	**776**
* Operational + in repair				

Sturmgeschütz brigades were subordinate field army command and deployed in support of corps and infantry divisions depending on the tactical circumstances. There were some experiments in subordinating the brigades directly to infantry divisions, notably StuG.Brigade.189 with the 78.Sturm-Division.

StuG brigades by army group, September 1, 1944				
	Brigades	**StuG**	**StuH**	**Total**
Nord	7	113+50*	40+15	**218**
Mitte	13	208+55	67+22	**352**
Nord-Ukraine	7	42+70	24+20	**156**
Sud-Ukraine	9	34	4	**38**
Subtotal		*397+175*	*135+57*	*532+232*
Total	**36****	**572**	**192**	**764**
*Operational + in repair				
**This total includes several battalions that totally lacked vehicles				

The Sturmgeschütz regularly could be found in two other types of units in Panzer and Panzergrenadier divisions as a tank-substitute, and in infantry anti-tank battalions.

A
PzKpfw IV IN OPERATION *BAGRATION*
1. PzKpfw IV Ausf H, 3./Panzer-Regiment.21, 20.Panzer-Division, Belarus, June 1944. This Vomag PzKpfw IV Ausf H was from the 3.Kompanie of Panzer-Regiment.21, evident from its tactical number of 301. It was knocked out during the fighting for the Bobruisk pocket at the end of June 1944 near the town of Zhlobin. The regimental insignia, a knight on a horse, can be seen on the front of the turret *Schurzen*. The standard camouflage pattern adopted in 1943 consisted of a base finish of RAL 7028 dark yellow, with patches of RAL 6003 olive green and RAL 8017 red brown applied by the unit in the field or depots issuing the tanks. This tank is fitted with a replacement gun barrel that is still in its factory dark-gray heat-resistant primer.

2. PzKpfw IV Ausf H, 4./Panzer-Regiment.21, 20.Panzer-Division, Belarus, June 1944. This Nibelungenwerke PzKpfw IV Ausf H of the commander of 4.Kompanie, Gerhard Glöckner, who was killed on June 27, 1944 during the fighting for the Bobruisk pocket while attempting to breakout of the village of Titovka. This tank is painted in the usual RAL 7028 dark yellow, with patches of RAL 6003 olive green and RAL 8017 red brown.

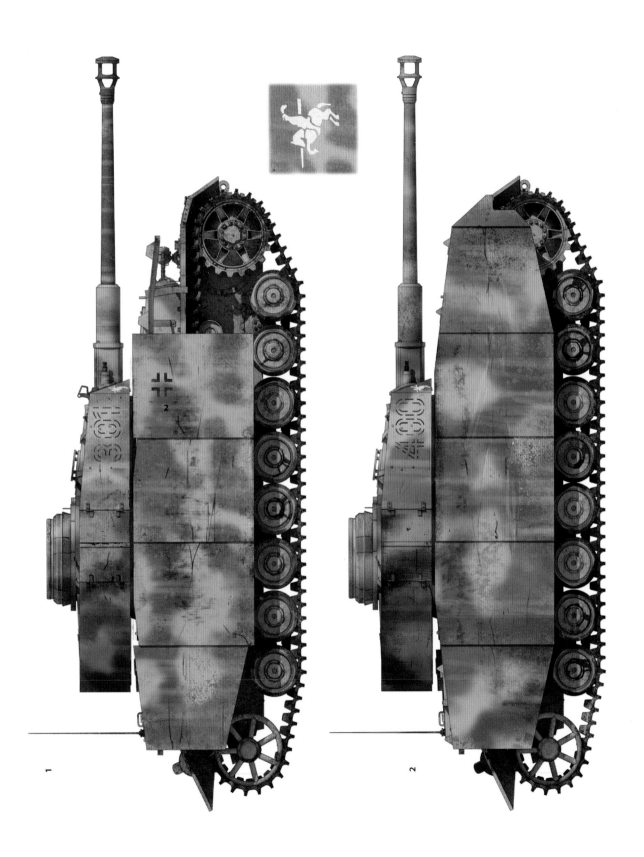

1

2

A Panther Ausf A tank of 2./Panzer-Rgt. Großdeutschland on September 21, 1944, at the conclusion of Operation *Cäsar*, a spoiling attack by 39.Panzerkorps south of Riga near Jelgava.

German infantry divisions had a Panzerjäger unit for anti-tank defense. Under the 1944 KStN for infantry divisions, there were four variations of this unit. The basic unit was a Panzerjäger company with 14 towed 7.5cm anti-tank guns. There were two other enhanced battalion configurations with three companies: a towed or self-propelled 2cm Flak company, an assault gun company with 10 StuG, and either a towed or self-propelled 7.5cm anti-tank gun company. A fourth variation substituted a self-propelled anti-tank gun company for the StuG company with 14 Panzerjäger vehicles. The self-propelled Panzerjäger was typically a Marder III 7.5cm PaK 40/3 although older types were still in use. There was a short-lived attempt to mount the 7.5cm PaK 40 anti-tank gun on the RSO tracked prime mover for this role, but after only 60 were built, the project was cancelled in June 1944 as a failure. Many of these served in infantry divisions of HG Nord.

Besides the infantry anti-tank units, there were also dedicated Panzerjäger units deployed at field army level. These were usually equipped with the Marder series. The older Marder II Pz.Jg. II 7.5cm PaK 40/2 was still in service in dwindling numbers with about 180 still in service on the Russian Front at the end of 1943. The most common type in the summer of 1944 was the Panzerjäger 38(t) 7.5cm PaK 40/3 Marder III. In June 1944, there were seven Panzerjäger-Abteilung on the Russian Front with 290 Panzerjäger 38 7.5cm PaK 40/3 of which 244 were ready and the rest in repair. The new Jagdpanzer 38 began appearing on the Russian Front in July 1944, first with the newly formed Heeres-Pz.Jg.Abt.731 in HG Nord and subsequently as replacements for the Marder III in Pz.Jg.Abt.743. During the summer of 1944, most Jagdpanzer 38 were assigned to the infantry tank destroyer units instead of the previous Marder series. The other new Jagdpanzer, the Jagdpanzer IV, was mainly issued to the Panzerjäger units of the Panzer divisions rather than to the separate battalions.

Hungarian school children romp over a StuG III Ausf G in the spring of 1944 when 3./StuG-Brigade.201 passed through the town of Községháza near Lake Balaton as part of Kampfgruppe Hillebrandt. The brigade was transferred to Poland in June 1944.

The heavy tank destroyer battalions (s.Pz.Jg.Abt.) were relatively rare and usually equipped with the 8.8cm Nashorn/Hornisse. These units had a nominal strength of 45 vehicles. A number of the Hornisse units active on the Russian Front in 1943 were returned to Germany in early 1944 to convert to the new Jagdpanther. Among the remaining Hornisse units on the Russian Front at the time of Operation *Bagration* were s.Pz. Jg.Abt.519 with HG Mitte, and s.Pz.Jg.Abt.88 with HG Nord-

Ukraine. There were no Jagdpanthers deployed on the Russian Front at the time of Operation *Bagration*.

The Wehrmacht operated a number of security (*Sicherungs*) and military police (*Ordnungspolizei*) units in the rear areas of the Russian Front to combat the extensive Soviet partisan movement. These units were equipped with obsolete German and war-booty tanks and armored cars.

There were also about 45 armored trains (*PZ: Panzerzüg*) operating in the rear areas of the Russian Front in 1944, primarily for defense of rail-lines and anti-partisan operations. The Wehrmacht generally operated its armored trains independently, but local commanders recommended following the Soviet practice of armored train battalions. The combined use of PZ 2 and PZ 68 at the Berezina river crossing near Shazliki in November 1943 promoted the formation of the first armored train regiments in 1944, each to consist of three battalions with two armored trains each. The plan was to consolidate the armored trains of each Heeresgruppe under these commands for better coordination. Under the chaotic conditions of the summer of 1944, this did not begin until the autumn of 1944.

Axis allies
Hungary
Hungary was Germany's only eastern ally to deploy a significant tank force following the start of Operation *Bagration*. Hungary was planning on exiting its alliance with Germany in the spring of 1944, prompting Hitler to launch Operation *Margarethe* in Budapest on March 19, 1944. Miklos Horthy was ousted and a puppet government under Prime Minister Dome Sztojay was installed. The Hungarian government was threatened with the introduction of Romanian and Slovak occupation troops if the *Honved* (Hungarian Army) did not remain allied to the Wehrmacht, so Hungary reluctantly continued participating in the war.

Under German pressure, the Honved deployed its 1st Army to eastern Galicia on the southeastern Polish–Ukrainian frontier in April 1944. This included the 2nd Armored Division and the new 1st Assault Gun Battalion. It was abundantly clear that Hungary's most modern tank, the Turan, was

The most powerful Panzerjäger in service in the early summer of 1944 was the 8.8cm PaK 43/41 *Hornisse* (Hornet), also sometimes called the *Nashorn* (Rhinoceros). They saw their combat debut on the Russian Front with s.Pz.Jg.Abt.655 in the summer of 1943.

A 7.5cm PaK 40 Panzerjäger Marder III takes up overwatch while a Hungarian Turan I medium tank advances forward during exercises in Galicia in April 1944. Hungary committed a larger tank force than any of Germany's eastern allies.

The Romanian army was so desperate for armored vehicles that it was forced to rely on improvisations such as the TACAM T-60. This consisted of captured Soviet T-60 light tanks with their turrets removed and a casemate added with captured Soviet F-22 76.2mm divisional guns. Seventeen of these were built in the summer of 1943 and they served in the Romanian 1st Armored Division.

completely inadequate against the newer Soviet tanks. During the short April 1944 counter-offensive, the division lost eight Turan I, nine Turan II, four Nimrod self-propelled guns, and one Toldi light tank while claiming to have knocked out 27 Soviet tanks. The local German commanders were impressed with the performance of the Hungarian tank units in these battles, and Generalfeldmarschall Walter Model, then commander of HG Nord Ukraine, ordered the transfer of a number of armored vehicles to reinforce the 2nd Armored Division. This included a few StuG III assault guns, ten PzKpfw IV Ausf H, and most surprisingly, ten Tiger heavy tanks of the s.Pz.Abt.503 which was in the process of conversion to the new Tiger II tank. These transfers were taken out of field stocks, and so do not usually show up in the official tallies of tanks transferred to Hungary later in the year. The Hungarian Tigers first went into action on July 26, 1944. By the middle of August 1944, the Hungarian 1st Army had been pushed back to the Hunyadi fortified line in the Carpathian Mountains on Hungary's eastern frontier.

The Hungarian 1st Cavalry Division was initially assigned on anti-partisan operations in eastern Poland/western Ukraine but following the *Bagration* offensive in June 1944, the division was sent forward in a vain attempt to stop the onrushing Soviet armored assault. In the fighting retreat from Kleck towards Brest-Litovsk, it lost nearly all of its armored vehicles including 84 Turan tanks. The Germans transferred a battery of Marder Panzerjäger to the division and it served in the August fighting around Warsaw. In September 1944, it was withdrawn back into Hungary where it was redesignated as the 1st Hussar Division.

Berlin finally agreed to transfer additional armored vehicles to Hungary starting in July 1944. By the end of 1944, this totaled 40 PzKpfw IV, five Panther tanks, 50 StuG III guns, and 35 Jagdpanzer 38. These did not see much fighting until the campaigns in Hungary late in the year.

Romania

The Romanian armored force was largely destroyed during the fighting around Stalingrad in 1942–43. Its surviving armored force was based around French Renault R-35 tanks, up-gunned with war-booty Soviet 45mm guns. There were small numbers of TACAM tank destroyers based on Czechoslovak R-2 light tanks and captured Soviet T-60 tanks, rearmed with war-booty Soviet 76mm guns. In the autumn of 1943, Berlin approved the Olivenbaum Program to rebuild the 1st "Great Romania" Armored Division and to create a new 2nd Armored Division. Between November

1943 and July 1944, Germany sold Romania a total of 116 PzKpfw IV tanks and 98 StuG III assault guns.

The Red Army reached Romanian soil in April–May 1944 during the first Iași-Chișinău offensive. The Romanian 1st Armored Division was heavily involved in the second battle for Iași-Chișinău in mid-August 1944 in separate battle-groups. On August 23, 1944, the king staged a *coup d'état* against the pro-German Antonescu regime and switched alliances to the Soviet side. A large number of German units located in Romania were forced to surrender and the Romanian army became allied to the Red Army.

The Finnish Army in 1944 relied on a mixture of captured Soviet tanks and StuG III assault guns purchased from Germany. This is a KV-1 that had been captured in the spring of 1942 and served in the Finnish Armored Division during the 1944 Karelian fighting. It is seen here in late 1943 at Äänislinna during trials of anti-tank obstacles. (SA-kuva)

Other Axis allies

The small Finnish armored force was equipped with a battalion of StuG III assault guns as well as an armored division equipped with war-booty Soviet types captured in 1941–44. Following the Soviet Karelian offensive in June 1944, Finland signed an armistice which obliged the army to expel German troops from Finland. German forces in Finland included some modest tank forces including Panzer-Abteilung.211 with war-booty Somua S-35 tanks.

Bulgaria was a nominal German ally, but never took part in any fighting against the Red Army. Starting in July 1943, Germany sold Bulgaria 46 PzKpfw IVs, 10 PzKpfw III tanks and 25 StuG III assault guns to modernize its 1st Armored Brigade. On September 9, 1944, Bulgaria switched sides. The 1st Armored Brigade served alongside the Red Army during the fighting in Hungary in 1945.

The Red Army

On January 1, 1944, the Red Army deployed 23 tank and mechanized corps, 46 tank and other armored brigades, and 106 tank and other armored regiments with 24,400 tanks and assault guns. About 40 percent of the Soviet armor was allotted to tank and assault gun units subordinate to infantry units to provide direct fire support during the penetration phase of the operation. A bit more than 60 percent of the armor was contained in the tank, mechanized, and cavalry units that would conduct the exploitation phase of the operation once the rifle corps had penetrated the German defensive belt. The units involved in Operation *Bagration* included eight tank and mechanized corps in addition to a substantial number of smaller brigades and regiments.

For major offensive operations, the Red Army organized several tank and mechanized corps along with smaller supporting formations into a tank army (*tankoviy armiya*). These were comparable to a German Panzer-Korps. These were temporary allotments though some corps were subordinated to tank armies for more than one campaign. The Red Army also created mechanized-cavalry groups that usually consisted of a cavalry corps and a mechanized corps. These were primarily intended for areas such as the Pripyat marshes that were not well-suited to motorized operations.

A T-34-85, probably from the 5th Guards Tank Army, 3rd Belarussian Front, knocked out in late June 1944 during fighting with the Tigers of s.Pz. Abt.505 along the Krupki–Minsk highway. The T-34-85 is armed with the D-5T gun in the configuration manufactured at Gorkiy Factory No. 112 in April 1944. Its gun is in full recoil which may have been the cause of its abandonment. Behind it is Tiger I number 301 of the staff section of 3./s.Pz.Abt.505.

The principal armored formations of the Red Army were the tank corps (TK: *tankoviy korpus*) and mechanized corps (MK: *mekhanizirovanniy korpus*). Although called corps, they were comparable to US or British divisions and were so re-named after the war.

The tank corps under the January 1944 *Shtat* (table of equipment) had three tank brigades, a motor rifle brigade, and three self-propelled assault gun regiments (light, medium, and heavy). This included 208 medium tanks, and 21 each of the SU-76, SU-85, and ISU-152. Some had an attached heavy tank regiment. The mechanized corps was similarly organized but with the balance of tank/motor rifle reversed. So the mechanized corps had three mechanized brigades and one tank brigade. Since the mechanized brigades each had an organic tank regiment, the corps had a substantial armored force including 21 light tanks, 176 medium tanks, and 21 each of the SU-76, SU-85, and ISU-152.

The Red Army's rifle divisions had no organic armor. Infantry tank support was provided by separate tank brigades (OTB: *otdelnaya tankovaya brigada*) and separate tank regiments (OTP: *otdelniy tankoviy polk*). Most tank brigades were equipped with T-34 or M4A2 medium tanks, though there were some heavy tank brigades (TTP: *tyzhëlaya tankovaya brigada*). Tank brigades under the usual November 1943 Shtat had three battalions of 21 tanks each for a total of 65 tanks per brigade including headquarters tanks. The brigades were usually subordinate to rifle corps for operations. The separate tank regiments were smaller, usually consisting of four tank companies totaling 41 tanks. These were generally subordinate to rifle divisions. The best known of the separate regiments was the Guards heavy tank breakthrough regiment (OGvTTP: *otdelniy gvardeiskiy tyazheliy tankoviy polk*) that was equipped with the new IS-2 heavy tanks. These began to be formed in February 1944 and had a total of 21 IS-2 tanks formed into four companies with five tanks each. Heavy tank regiments not given the Guards honorific were designated as separate breakthrough tank regiments (*otdelniy tankoviy polk proryva*). A few tank regiments were configured as engineer tank regiments, equipped with flame-thrower tanks and mine-clearing tanks. Most of these belonged to the specialist engineer assault brigades (*Shturmovaya inzhenerno-sapernaya brigada*).

Self-propelled artillery was organized much like the separate tank units: the self-propelled artillery brigade (SABr: *samokhodnaya-artilleriyskaya brigada*) and self-propelled artillery regiment (SAP: *samokhodniy-artilleriyskiy polk*). These were distinguished by the type of equipment they used, whether the light SU-76 (*leghkiy*), medium SU-85 (*sredniy*), or heavy SU-152/ISU-122/ISU-152 (*tyzëliy*). The April 1943 Shtat for the light SPG regiment contained 21 SU-76, organized as five batteries with four SU-76 each, plus a single SU-76 in the headquarters. This was supplemented with the smaller separate SP artillery battalions (OSAD: *Otdelniy samokhodniy artilleriskiy divizion*) initially

A battery of SU-76M assault guns of the 1st Belarussian Front on July 16, 1944, during the summer 1944 offensive.

consisting of three batteries, each with four SU-76M. These units were designed to be directly attached to rifle divisions for fire support, rather than concentrating them at corps or field army level. The first 11 of these units were formed in April 1944, followed by 40 more in September 1944. The new February 1944 Shtat for the medium and heavy regiments standardized the regimental organization of all self-propelled gun regiments to 21 vehicles; previously the medium regiment had 16 SU-85 and the heavy regiment had only 12 SU-152.

Assault gun brigades were generally deployed for corps support while the regiments were frequently subordinate to rifle divisions. Unlike the Wehrmacht, the Red Army did not make a distinction between assault gun and tank destroyer units. All were simply called self-propelled artillery (*samokhodnaya artilleriya*) even though the medium types such as the SU-85 were clearly oriented to the tank destroyer role.

There were a handful of armored car battalions. This was an archaic formation dating back to the 1930s when the Red Army was still using

The PT-3 mine-roller was developed in 1943 to hastily breach mine-fields. It entered Red Army service in April 1943 and was first used in combat at Kursk in July 1943. This is an example fitted to a T-34 tank of the Polish People's Army (LWP).

The Soviet OT-34-76 flamethrower tank was equipped with an ATO-42 flamethrower in place of the usual hull machine gun. These were assigned to special tank flamethrower regiments for assaulting German fortified lines. A total of 489 of these were built in 1943–44 at Factory No. 174 in Omsk. This example with the tactical number D-44 was knocked out in the summer 1944 fighting and is seen being examined by German troops.

medium armored cars such as the BA-10. They were mostly found on the Leningrad Front which had been surrounded for much of the war. As a result, this front still operated obsolete vehicles from 1941.

The Red Army made extensive use of armored trains through the war. The road network in much of the Soviet Union was poor and railroads provided the most important arteries of transportation. While the Wehrmacht tended to use their armored trains defensively for protection of communication lines and anti-partisan operations, the Red Army continued to use armored trains as offensive units. They were usually deployed in battalions (*Otdelniy divizion bronepoezdov*) with two trains plus technical support. The main role of the armored train was to provide either direct or indirect fire support akin to a rail-bound self-propelled gun battery. However, they could also be used in mobile missions by including a dismount (*desantniy*) infantry unit to help seize key objectives such as railway stations and bridges. The use of armored trains generally declined once the front-lines reached the Soviet border in the summer of 1944, because it was time-consuming to convert the trains from the Soviet railroad gauge to the European gauge.

The accompanying chart shows the number of the major Red Army armored formations at the beginning of January 1945. It is arranged

B

SU-85 IN OPERATION *BAGRATION*

1. SU-85, 1047th Self-Propelled Artillery Regiment, 67th Army, 3rd Baltic Front, summer 1944. This SU-85 has the tactical number 801 and the patriotic slogan "*Smert' nemetskim okkupantam!*" ("Death to the German Occupiers"). The unit insignia was a "K" on a shield. It also has a pair of stars on either side of the tactical number.

2. SU-85, 1443rd Self-propelled Artillery Regiment, 23rd Tank Corps, 2nd Ukrainian Front, Romania, August 1944. This SU-85 is finished in the usual 4BO camouflage green with the tactical number S-13. The 23rd Tank Corps usually used a rhomboid insignia about 400mm high as its tactical symbol with a letter inside for the sub-unit: V (3rd Tank Brigade), G (39th Tank Brigade), and D (135th Tank Brigade). A number was painted in the lower right to identify the battalion. So V₁ as shown here in Cyrillic script (**2a**) indicated the 1st Battalion, 3rd Tank Brigade. For some reason, the corps' SP regiment did not follow this practice, but used a large letter without the rhomboid, in this case "S", to identify the regiment (a Cyrillic "S" appears like a Roman "C" as seen on the plate).

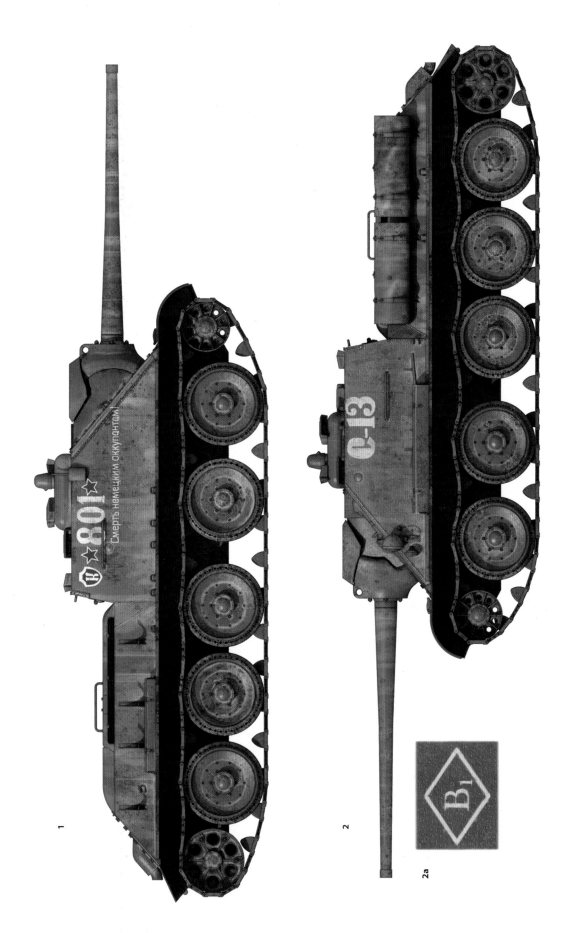

1

2

2a

geographically starting with the Karelian Front in the north. Red Army Fronts were roughly comparable to US or British field armies.

Soviet tank and AFV units at the front, July 1, 1944								
Fronts	TK	MK	OTBr	OTP	SABr	SAP	OABrB	OBrP
Karelian			3	7		6		3
Leningrad			4	14		13	4	7
3rd Baltic			2	4		3	1	
2nd Baltic	1		3	5		4		5
1st Baltic	1		5	6		9		2
3rd Belorussian	3	1	4	6		13		2
2nd Belorussian			4	1		10		2
1st Belorussian	6	1	2	14	2	29		5
1st Ukrainian	7	3	4	8		7	1	7
2nd Ukrainian	3	2	1	2	1	1		5
3rd Ukrainian		1	1	2		5		3
4th Ukrainian	1	3		1	1	7		
Total	**22**	**11**	**33**	**70**	**4**	**107**	**6**	**41**

Legend:

TK = *Tankoviy korpus,* Tank corps

MK = *Mekhanizirovanniy korpus,* Mechanized corps

OTBr = *Otdelnaya tankovaya brigada,* Separate tank brigade

OTP = *Otdelniy tankoviy polk,* Separate tank regiment

SABr = *Samokhodnaya artilleriskaya brigada,* SP artillery brigade

SAP = *Samokhodniy artilleriskiy polk,* SP artillery regiment

OABrB = *Otdelniy avtobronevoy batalon,* Separate armored car battalion

OBrP = *Otdelniy Bronepoezd,* Separate armored train

T-34 tanks of the Polish People's Army 2nd Tank Regiment, 1st Armored Brigade are loaded on a barge to cross the Vistula river near Magnuszew on August 10, 1944. The rear tank, number 236 of Warrant Officer J. Kulesza, carries the jeep of political commissar Capt. J. Tokarski. Both tanks are the late 1943 configuration with the Gayka turret and commander's cupola, built at Gorkiy Factory No. 112 in September 1943.

Red Army allies
Poland
The Red Army began organizing the Polish People's Army (LWP: *Ludowe Wojsko Polskie*) in the Soviet Union in the spring of 1943. These units were identical in composition and equipment to Soviet units and much of the officer cadre came from the Red Army. By the time of the 1944 summer campaign, the Polish forces had grown to a field army, the 1 *Armia Polska*, that had armored elements including the 1st Armored Brigade, the 13th SP Regiment with the SU-85, and four light SU-76 SP battalions attached to its four infantry divisions. These formations were attached to the 1st Belorussian Front during the summer 1944 campaigns. The Polish Home Army insurgents captured a small number of German armored vehicles during the Warsaw Uprising including a few Panther tanks.

Romania
When Romania switched sides on August 23, 1944, some Romanian armored vehicles from the army training center were deployed as the Niculescu Armored Detachment and were

involved in skirmishes with German troops in Bucharest during the coup. The 1st Armored (Training) Division saw some fighting in the Otopeni and Băneasa areas as well. In September 1944, the 1st and 4th Romanian Armies were put under Soviet command. The 2nd Tank Regiment with about 66 PzKpfw IV and R-35/45 tanks, and 80 other armored vehicles took part in later fighting in the Balkans, Austria, and Czechoslovakia alongside the Red Army in 1944–45.

TECHNICAL FACTORS

Wehrmacht

The Wehrmacht attempted to counteract the larger number of Soviet tanks by adopting technically superior tanks. Since 1941, the Wehrmacht attempted to replace the older PzKpfw III and PzKpfw IV tanks with newer designs, notably the Panther tank. This proved to be impossible due to the limitations of German industry and the relatively low priority afforded to the Panzer industry. Panzer production amounted to only about four percent of the German weapons production in 1942. In September 1942, Hitler demanded that more resources be put into armored vehicle manufacture, doubling it to an eight percent share. In September 1942, he established a goal of 1,200 AFVs per month by the end of 1944. Of these, 800 were to be tanks and of those, 600 Panthers and 50 Tigers. To put this in perspective, German tank production in September 1942 was 325 tanks per month plus a further 120 assault guns and tank destroyers for a total of 445. Soviet tank production at the time was about five times as high, 2,100 tanks per month. German tank and AFV production closed the gap in 1944 averaging 1,480 monthly compared to the Soviet tank and AFV production of 2,280 monthly, or roughly a 1:1.5 Soviet advantage. During fighting on the Russian Front from December 1943 to May 1944, the Wehrmacht lost 2,674 tanks, 1,616 StuG assault guns, and 572 Panzerjäger tank destroyers for a total of 4,862.

Another major change in 1943 was the shift to manufacture more AFVs other than tanks. The General Inspector of the Panzer Force, and later army chief-of-staff, Heinz Guderian, had attempted to monopolize industrial resources for tank production to the exclusion of other AFVs aimed at infantry support, notably assault guns (*Sturmgeschütz*).

A column of PzKpfw IV Ausf H on a road march during the late spring 1944 fighting.

The Panther tank finally arrived on the Russian Front in the summer of 1943 during the battle of Kursk. It was a technical embarrassment due to lingering mechanical immaturity. Most of these problems were ironed out by early 1944 with the advent of the Panther Ausf A, but Panther production remained far below expectations. The intention had been to deploy an equal mix of PzKpfw IV and Panther tank battalions in the Panzer divisions by the summer of 1944. However, shortages of new Panther tanks and the priority assigned to the Normandy Front meant that only about 25 percent

A pair of Panther Ausf A tanks of 4./Panzer-Rgt. Großdeutschland of Panzergrenadier-Division Großdeutschland, probably during training exercises in Romania in June 1944. The division fought along the East Prussian border in August 1944.

of the tank strength in Panzer divisions on the Russian Front was made up of Panthers and 56 percent of PzKpfw IV. In contrast, 37 percent of the tanks in Normandy were Panthers and 60 percent were PzKpfw IV. There were still a significant number of PzKpfw III in service on the Russian Front in the summer of 1944, almost 17 percent, while there were very few in Normandy. In mid-June 1944, there were actually more Tiger I tanks than Panthers.

In spite of these manufacturing problems, the Wehrmacht continued to enjoy a significant technological edge in tank performance in the summer of 1944. The PzKpfw IV Ausf H was still superior to the T-34 in firepower and neither type enjoyed a clear advantage in either mobility or armored protection. The newly arrived T-34-85 was close to the PzKpfw IV in firepower when firing standard armor-piercing ammunition, but superior when using the new HVAP (High Velocity Armor Piercing) with a tungsten carbide core. Although the Wehrmacht had developed 7.5cm HVAP ammunition, it was extremely rare on the battlefield in 1944 due to severe shortages of tungsten carbide.

The Panther tank was significantly superior to the T-34-85 in terms of firepower, armored protection, and mobility. A post-war Soviet technical comparison of the wartime vehicles reached the assessment shown in the accompanying chart. The PzKpfw III Ausf L/M was chosen as the baseline for the comparison and its technical features valued at 1. The other types were then evaluated accordingly. The Soviet study suggested that the combat value of the Panther compared to the T-34-85 was almost double.

Comparative combat value 1944				
PzKpfw III	T-34	PzKpfw IV	T-34-85	Panther
1.0	1.16	1.27	1.32	2.37

The Tiger I heavy tank remained the single best tank in combat in the summer of 1944. In 1943, it was invulnerable to Soviet tank gun fire in the frontal arc since both the T-34 and KV tanks were limited to the 76mm

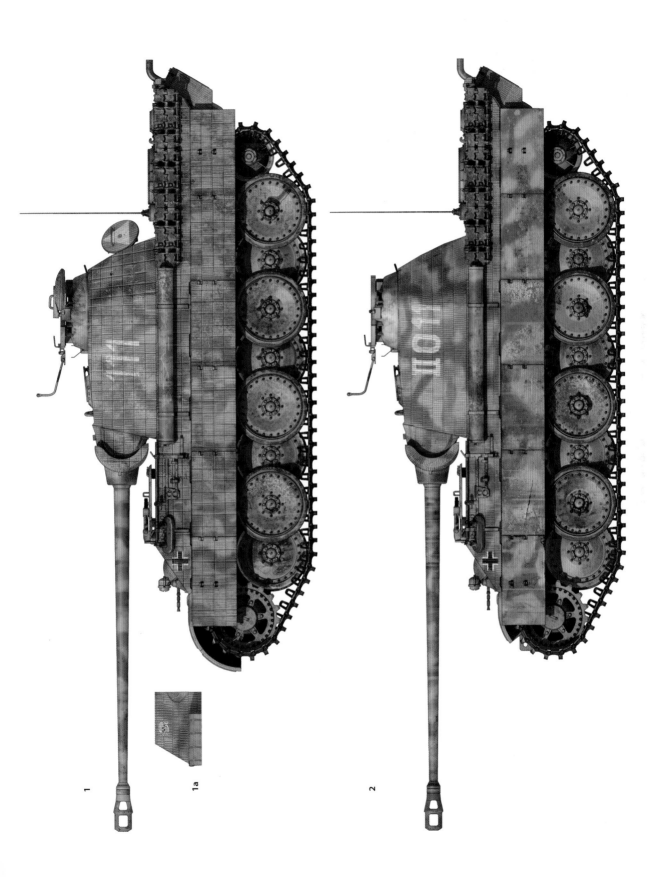

1

1a

2

On August 18, 1944, SS-Pz. Rgt.5 "Wiking" attempted to counter-attack Soviet forces northeast of Warsaw, but ran into elements of the 8th Guards Tank Corps between Tłuszcz and Jasienica. This Panther Ausf A of 8.Kompanie became bogged in an irrigation ditch, and may have been one of three Panthers later recovered and put back into use by the corps.

gun. By 1944, the advent of the 85mm gun on the T-34-85 and the 122mm gun on the IS-2 ended the Tiger's frontal invulnerability. Even if the Tiger was not as omnipotent in 1944 as it was in 1943, it was still one of the best in tank-vs-tank combat. Its two main failings were the small number of tanks available at any one time due to its high production cost, and a relatively low availability rate due to its high maintenance demands. Berlin attempted to improve the situation by providing more spare parts in the spring of 1944, and by June 1944 it reached its peak availability rate of 73 percent. However, once high intensity combat resumed in July 1944, this fell to 60 percent in July and 48 percent in August.

Its successor, the Tiger II, debuted on the Russian Front in August 1944. In spite of its superior firepower and armor, it was a clumsy and overweight design. The Tiger II was symptomatic of the German failure to moderate technological extremism in the face of persistent Panzer shortages.

German AFV readiness rates (percent) on Russian Front by type in 1944				
	Jun	Jul	Aug	Sep
StuG III	85	75	65	71
Pz III	69	68	63	60
Pz IV	84	73	60	63
Panther	80	73	51	60
Tiger	75	60	48	64

The most important German armored vehicle on the Russian Front in the summer of 1944 was the StuG III assault gun and its related types such as the StuH 42 with the 10.5cm howitzer. These assault guns outnumbered all German tanks combined. Furthermore, their durability compared to the troublesome Panther and Tiger tanks meant that the StuG was the predominant Wehrmacht armored vehicle on the Russian Front from August 1943 through the end of the war. Guderian had tried to suppress StuG production in favor of Panzer production, but its combat effectiveness combined with its low cost led to steady increases in production. The StuG III used the production resources previously allotted to the obsolete PzKpfw III tank, but armed with the same 7.5cm gun as the PzKpfw IV tank. Its combat effectiveness was improved by other factors, including the use of better sights and the more extensive gunnery training of StuG crews by the artillery branch.

A Tiger I number 124 of s.Pz. Abt.510 supporting troops of the 21.Luftwaffe-Feld-Division near Akmenė, Lithuania, in late August 1944.

When the main StuG manufacturer, Alkett, was bombed by the RAF in October 1943, Hitler authorized the switch from PzKpfw IV production at Krupp to the StuG IV. This was essentially a slightly modified StuG III superstructure mated to a PzKpfw IV chassis. This entered production in December 1943 but remained overshadowed by the more numerous StuG III.

The StuG essentially became the Wehrmacht's infantry tank. Even though it was not intended for tank fighting, this became an increasing share of its mission by 1943. From June 1941 through August 1944, Sturmgeschütz units claimed 18,261 kills against Soviet AFVs. Total German claims against Soviet AFVs including claims by tanks, anti-tank guns, and close-attack infantry weapons totaled 100,748, so the StuG claims represented nearly a fifth (18 percent) of all claims. However, the StuG's main mission was direct fire support of the infantry, and about 85 percent of its ammunition consumption was high-explosive projectiles for this mission.

Comparative German AFV production by type 1941–44							
	Panzer	(%)	Sturmgeschütz	(%)	Panzerjäger	(%)	Total
1941	3,256	85.7	540	14.2	0	0	3,796
1942	4,278	69.5	748	12.1	1,123	18.2	6,149
1943	5,966	55.5	3,406	31.6	1,375	12.7	10,747
1944	9,161	50.1	8,682	47.4	441	2.4	18,284

The relative proportion of Panzerjäger production declined from 1943 to 1944. This was in part due to the growing role of the StuG in the anti-tank role. Most Panzerjäger production in 1942–43 consisted of the adaptation of the obsolete PzKpw 38(t) light tank into the Marder series armed with various guns in the 7.5cm range. Although these were more effective than towed 7.5cm PaK 40 guns, they were modestly armored with an open fighting compartment making the gun crew extremely vulnerable to small arms fire and enemy artillery. A variety of newer vehicles began to replace them in 1944. Curiously enough, the replacements stemmed from an effort to replace the StuG III.

The "*Sturmgeschütz neuer Art*" was the Sd Kfz 162 based on the PzKpfw IV chassis. Unlike the StuG IV, this mounted the same 7.5cm gun in a new, simplified casemate with better frontal armor. In the event, Guderian's Panzer inspectorate recommended its production as the Jagdpanzer IV, intended for the Panzerjäger units of the Panzer force, not as assault guns for the infantry. It was something of a waste to use a PzKpfw IV chassis with the same gun as the tank version, and later in 1944, a more effective version was developed which added the longer L/70 gun of the Panther tank. This became the Panzer IV/70.

The next "*Sturmgeschütz neuer Art*" was an attempt to convert the two tank plants in the Czech provinces to a fully enclosed 7.5cm gun instead of the exposed gun of the Marder series. The result was something of a mixed bag. The Jagdpanzer 38, unofficially called the "*Hetzer*," offered excellent frontal armor. However, the side armor was only proof against small arms fire. The interior was so cramped that the ergonomic layout of the fighting compartment was very poor.

A StuG III Ausf G named "*Sperber*" (sparrow hawk) of StuG-Brigade.202 on August 31, 1944. The brigade fought in the Kurland region of the Baltic in the late summer and autumn of 1944. This vehicle was from Alkett's May/June 1944 production batch. Some units mounted the rear maintenance hatches on the bow for extra armor, as seen here.

A pair of StuG knocked out during the summer fighting. The vehicle to the right is the normal StuG III Ausf G with 7.5cm gun while the vehicle to the left is a 10.5cm Sturmhaubitze 42.

The commander in particular had a hard time directing the vehicle in combat due to poor provisions for vision devices. In spite of the intention to use the vehicle as a cheap supplement to the StuG III, Guderian once again intervened and called it a Jagdpanzer. The first vehicles deployed on the Russian Front in July 1944 went to Panzerjäger battalions, but they were viewed as distinctly inferior to the Jagdpanzer IV. As a result, through the end of 1944, most were assigned instead to the Panzerjäger units in infantry divisions.

There were a number of heavy Panzerjäger types in service in 1944, though only the Nashorn/Hornisse was common on the Russian Front in the summer of 1944. The Hornisse consisted of a modified PzKpfw IV chassis armed with a 8.8cm Pak 43/41 in an open rear compartment. Due to the extremely powerful gun, the battalions equipped with these vehicles used them from stand-off distances to minimize their vulnerability to close infantry attack. In terms of the kill/loss ratios, the Hornisse was one of the most effective German AFVs on the Russian Front, but they were very few in number.

The 90 8.8cm Ferdinand/Elefant were also designated as a Sturmgeschütz but were assigned to two heavy Panzerjäger battalions for the battle of Kursk. They had mixed results and were withdrawn for reconstruction. Two companies were assigned to s.Pz.Jg.Abt.653 and took part in the fighting in Ukraine during the summer of 1944; the rest served in Italy. The Jagdpanther, a version of the Panther tank with an 8.8cm gun in a fixed casemate, entered service in the Normandy campaign but did not appear on the Russian Front until after the summer 1944 battles.

The most common version of the T-34 during Operation *Bagration* was this configuration with the *Gayka* (hex nut) turret. Although a commander's cupola for this turret was introduced in the autumn of 1943, many tanks still used the earlier configuration with "Mickey Mouse" hatches.

Red Army

There was a substantial change in the Soviet tank force since the summer 1943 battles. The reliance on the 76mm gun and the appearance of the heavily armored Panther and Tiger tanks forced the Red Army to pay more attention to firepower. This resulted in the new T-34-85 medium tank and IS-2 heavy tank. In addition, Soviet light tank production ended in favor of using these resources to manufacture the SU-76M assault gun. During the summer 1944 campaigns, the Red Army's armored force consisted of about 70 percent tanks and 30 percent self-propelled guns.

Production of light tanks, including the T-70 and T-80, ended in August 1943 in favor of the SU-76M assault gun. At the start of 1944, the Red Army had 21,100 tanks on hand, of which 10,300 (49%) were light tanks including the T-70, Lend-Lease types such as the Valentine, and a wide range of obsolete tanks. The March 1944 Shtat for tank regiments dropped the light tank company. The T-70 and Valentine remained in service in small numbers in self-propelled gun units and motorcycle regiments as command tanks. As a result, light tanks became increasingly uncommon on the 1944 battlefield and were relegated to training roles, or with units outside the main theaters.

Light tanks in the tank armies, summer 1944			
	T-60	T-70	Valentine
1st Tank Army			9
2nd Tank Army			10
3rd Tank Army	3	3	5

The standard T-34 medium tank at the end of 1943 was the configuration with the 76mm gun in the *Gayka* (hex nut) turret. Starting in August 1943, a portion of these tanks received a new commander's cupola that improved the commander's situational awareness. The main improvement in this tank was an initiative by the main T-34 plant, Nizhi-Tagil's Factory No. 183, to improve reliability. This was a series of standardized upgrades to sub-assemblies and improved quality control. T-34 tanks had a nominal warrantied life of 330km without major breakdown, but factory tests in 1943 found that this objective was woefully unfulfilled with only 37 percent of the tanks reaching this standard. By December 1943–February 1944, it had risen to 82 percent.

The most significant change in combat value came with the adoption of the new 85mm tank gun. Initially, a small number of tanks were built at the Gorkiy plant with the D-5 gun as used on the SU-85 tank destroyer. This gun had an excessively large breach and was gradually replaced at Gorkiy with the S-53 gun, better suited to a turret interior. The ultimate version was the ZIS-S-53, and this gun was introduced when Nizhni-Tagil switched to T-34-85 production in March 1944. The T-34-85 also introduced a new three-man turret that improved the combat effectiveness of the tank by allowing the tank commander to concentrate on leading the tank and not being distracted servicing the gun. The T-34 with 76mm gun remained in production in declining numbers at Omsk until September 1944, at which time all three T-34 plants were exclusively manufacturing the T-34-85 as shown in the accompanying chart.

A T-34 Factory No. 174 Omsk production of the 3rd Baltic Front leads a column through Vilnius, the Lithuanian capital, on July 14, 1944. The device on the front of the tank is the frame for a PT-3 mine-roller. To the side are some Lend-Lease GPA amphibious jeeps, a popular vehicle in Red Army reconnaissance units.

| Transition of T-34 production to 85mm gun in 1944 | | | | | | | | | |
Plant	Jan	Feb	Mar	Apr	May	Jun	Jul	Aug	Sep
T-34									
Nizhni-Tagil	645	680	513						
Gorkiy	240	165	135						
Omsk	150	150	166	176	186	177	102	154	2
Chelyabinsk	185	185	75						
T-34-85									
Nizhni-Tagil			150	696	701	706	711	714	723
Gorkiy	25	75	178	296	300	315	315	315	315
Omsk						13	93	146	198
Sub-total, T-34	*25*	*75*	*328*	*992*	*1,001*	*1,034*	*1,119*	*1,175*	*1,236*
Sub-total, T-34-85	*1,220*	*1,180*	*889*	*176*	*186*	*177*	*102*	*154*	*2*
Total	**1,245**	**1,255**	**1,217**	**1,168**	**1,187**	**1,211**	**1,221**	**1,329**	**1,238**

The other medium tank in service in the summer of 1944 was the Lend-Lease M4A2 Sherman. It was incorporated into separate tank regiments, separate tank brigades, and the sub-units of the larger tank and mechanized corps. For example, the 8th Guards Tank Corps during the advance on Lublin, Poland, in July 1944 had 42–44 M4A2 tanks in each of its three component brigades, plus 23–32 T-34 tanks.

Production of the KV heavy tank ended in 1943 in favor of a new heavy tank. The principal options for the new tank were a 100mm or 122mm gun. Although the 100mm gun offered better anti-tank performance, the Red Army viewed its heavy tanks as breakthrough tanks intended to support the rifle divisions. The 122mm gun derived from the common A-19 field gun that fired a massive 25kg (55lb) high-explosive projectile. This was six times heavier than the Panther's 4kg round and three times heavier than the Tiger's 9kg round. As a result, the 122mm gun was selected, with the new tank initially being called the IS-122 (IS: *Iosef Stalin*), and later as the IS-2. The main drawback of the 122mm gun was its two-piece field artillery ammunition which reduced the rate of fire and limited the on-board ammunition to only 28 rounds. The first IS tanks were completed by the end of 1943 and the first separate Guards heavy tank regiments were formed in February 1944. A Soviet institute later estimated the relative combat value of the principal Soviet types as shown in the accompanying chart in which the T-34 was assigned as the baseline, valued at "1."

| Comparative combat value of Soviet AFVs 1944–45 | | | |
SU-76M	T-34	T-34-85	IS-2
0.74	1.0	1.14	1.62

The most numerically significant Soviet AFV in 1944 after the T-34 tank was the SU-76M assault gun. This program served the dual purpose of providing the infantry with additional firepower and better utilizing the limited production capacities of the light tank plants. The SU-76M consisted of a lengthened T-70 light tank chassis fitted with an open rear compartment armed with the ZiS-3 76mm gun. Although this weapon is often misidentified as an anti-tank gun, it was in fact the Red Army's standard divisional field gun, performing the same role as the 25pdr in the British Army or the 105mm howitzers in the Wehrmacht and US Army.

The SU-76M had many shortcomings due to its cheap construction and small size. It was ill-suited to close combat support since its armor was thin and its rear fighting compartment completely exposed to enemy small arms fire, grenades, mortar fire, and overhead artillery airbursts. It was widely nicknamed as "*Suka*" in the Red Army, which can be translated either as "Little SU" or as "Bitch." In spite of its shortcomings, it provided the Red Army with a large volume of mobile guns for offensive operations.

The Red Army also operated a small number of tank destroyer units based on Lend-Lease equipment in 1944. The Red Army received 650 T48 57mm gun motor carriages, renaming them as the SU-57-I (I = *innostranniy*, foreign). They were deployed in separate tank destroyer brigades with a total of 60 SU-57-Is each. They saw their combat debut in August 1943 on a scale of one brigade per tank army. The SU-57 was also deployed in separate motorcycle battalions.

T-34-85 tanks of the 36th Guards Tank Brigade, 4th Guards Mechanized Corps, 3rd Ukrainian Front east of the Moldovan town of Bender during the fighting along the Dnestr river in May 1944. The tanks are from the spring 1944 production series at Gorkiy Factory No. 112 with the S-53 gun.

The Red Army also received 52 M10 3in. GMC tank destroyers that were used to form two self-propelled artillery regiments. The 1223rd SP Regiment served with the 29th Tank Corps of the 5th Guards Tank Army, 3rd Belorussian Front, in the fighting in 1944 in Belarus. The 1239th SPA Regiment served with the 16th Tank Corps of the 2nd Tank Army, 1st Belarussian Front, in the 1944 campaigns in Belarus and Poland.

The standard medium self-propelled gun in 1944 was the SU-85 consisting of a T-34 hull with a D-5S 85mm gun mounted in a fixed casemate. The 85mm gun offered anti-tank performance comparable to the 75mm gun on the German PzKpfw IV Ausf H. It was an expedient method to arm the T-34 with a more powerful gun than the 76mm. Once the T-34-85 appeared, the SU-85's days were numbered since a more powerful 100mm gun was desired. However, the SU-100 did not appear in time for the 1944 summer battles.

This new T-34-85 of the 25th Guards Tank Brigade, 2nd Guards Tank Corps was knocked out in Nemmersdorf during the bitter fighting in East Prussia in October 1944, the first Soviet attack on German soil.

There were several heavy self-propelled guns in service in the summer of 1944. The older SU-152 was deployed in dwindling numbers since production had ended in 1943. It was replaced by the ISU-152 that switched from the KV to the IS chassis, though armed with the same 152mm gun. The ISU-152 was supplemented by the ISU-122 later in 1944, armed with the A-19 or D-25 guns. There was no tactical difference between the ISU-122 and ISU-152 but any variation was primarily based on the availability of gun tubes and ammunition. Both types were intended for direct fire support

An IS-2 of the 13th Guards Heavy Tank Regiment, 2nd Baltic Front, during the fighting with Heeregruppe Nord east of Riga, Latvia in September 1944.

during breakthrough operations. They have a reputation of being powerful tank destroyers, but this was a secondary mission and not their main role.

THE CAMPAIGN

The summer campaign of 1944 on the Russian Front was shaped by the successes and failure of the previous winter and spring campaigns of the Red Army. After halting the German offensive against the Kursk salient in the summer of 1943, the Red Army took the strategic initiative in the subsequent year of fighting. By January 1944, the Wehrmacht had been comprehensively defeated across the Russian Front, but Soviet progress had been decidedly uneven. In the north, the siege of Leningrad was finally lifted at the end of January 1944, but the Wehrmacht was firmly ensconced in the neighboring Baltic region, which shielded Germany's most exposed eastern province of East Prussia. Fighting on the approaches to Leningrad continued through March 1944 to clear German forces from the area and to liberate the city of Novgorod.

In the center, *Heeresgruppe Mitte* (Army Group Center) had continued to frustrate the Red Army's attempts to advance into Belarus. The Red Army had

D SHERMANS IN OPERATION *BAGRATION*

1. M4A2, 32nd Tank Regiment, 16th Guards Cavalry Division, 7th Guards Cavalry Corps, Poland, July 1944. Each of the three cavalry divisions in the 7th Guards Cavalry Corps had a tank regiment. The insignia appears to have been a yellow horseshoe with the regimental number inside though details are lacking. The tanks carried the usual three-digit tactical number and it is possible that the first digit identified the division/tank regiment in sequence. These Lend-Lease M4A2 remained in overall US Army olive drab, evident from the fact that the white shipping stencils were still evident on the side.

2. M4A2, 59th Guards Tank Brigade, 8th Guards Tank Corps, Poland, July 1944. The 8th Guards Tank Corps had a distinctive unit insignia consisting of a tombstone shape with a large white circle inside. The first number of the three-digit tactical number appears to have indicated the tank units within the corps with the IS-2 tanks of the 62nd Guards Breakthrough Regiment starting in "5" and the Guards tank brigades (58, 59, 60 GTB) using "6" through "8."

An SU-76M assault gun in the foothills of the Carpathian Mountains during the 1st Ukrainian Front offensive in the summer of 1944.

German troops inspect an SU-85 assault gun of the 1021st Self-propelled Artillery regiment, 11th Tank Destroyer Artillery Brigade near Devindoni, Lithuania on July 30, 1944, during the Šiauliai offensive. The regiment was positioned behind the towed 57mm guns of the 747th Anti-tank Artillery Regiment when struck by a major German counter-attack. The SU-85s were credited with knocking out 19 German AFVs that day.

staged a series of offensives since October 1943 to push back the Wehrmacht and to liberate the capital, Minsk. These offensives failed due to the weather, terrain, and stubborn German defenses.

The most savage tank battles of early winter 1943 and spring 1944 were fought in Ukraine. The campaign for Right-Bank Ukraine started during the final week of December 1943 after the Red Army had liberated the capital, Kiev. The operational objective was to clear the area west of the Dnieper river as well as German hold-outs in Crimea. Hitler's demands that the Wehrmacht not withdraw from the Dnieper defense lines led to a series of costly encirclement battles including the Korsun-Shevchenkovskiy salient. The sequential Red Army offensives continued through mid-April 1944 with the Red Army reaching the Carpathian Mountains near the Polish and Romanian frontiers. The success of the Right-Bank campaign placed the Red Army's southern tier of forces about 300km further west than those in the north and center. These offensives came at a heavy toll with the December 1943–April 1944 battles, costing the Red Army 4,666 tanks and AFVs. The final spring 1944 campaign retook the Crimean peninsula in April–May.

In March 1944, Stalin and the Soviet high command began plans for the summer 1944 operations. The advances in Ukraine opened the possibilities for a north-westward thrust through southern Poland to the Baltic, or a south-westward plunge into Romania and the Balkans. The Wehrmacht expected the Red Army attack in this sector due to its strategic opportunities, as well as the momentum built up in the previous Ukrainian offensives. However, a Soviet thrust from Ukraine would leave the northern flanks exposed to German counter-attacks from HG Mitte and HG Nord. An attack from Belarus had the twin advantages of clearing the Wehrmacht from occupied Soviet lands while at the same time opening the shortest and most direct route to Berlin.

A major factor in planning the summer 1944 offensive was the Anglo-American promise to stage an amphibious invasion of France in May 1944.

The threat of this invasion forced the Wehrmacht to shift substantial forces from east to west through the spring of 1944. This was most evident in Panzer units. Hitler hoped that a concentrated Panzer attack on the Allied invasion site would push Anglo-American forces back into the Channel. Such a defeat would permit the Wehrmacht to shift critical Panzer forces back to the Russian Front in time to resist the expected Soviet summer campaign. This was wishful thinking.

Until 1944, the bulk of the Panzer force was deployed on the Russian

Front. For example, in July 1943, there were 1,989 operational tanks of which 1,265 tanks (63%) were deployed on the Russian Front, 382 (19%) were in the West, mainly in Italy or in France for training, and 342 (17%) in the *Heimat* (Homeland) for unit reconstruction. In 1944, the balance began to shift in favor of the Western Front so that by May 1944, Panzer strength in the West exceeded the Russian Front for the first time since 1940. The shift west included most of the Waffen-SS Panzer divisions including the 1, 2, 9, 10, and 12.SS-Panzer Divisionen.

German operational tank strength 1944: East vs West					
	May	**Jun**	**Jul**	**Aug**	**Sep**
East	1,044	1,244	1,511	1,691	1,485
West	1,654	1,797	2,014	1,723	1,534
Homeland	1,157	1,011	9,83	874	846
Total	**3,855**	**4,052**	**4,508**	**4,288**	**3,865**

Starved of Panzer reserves, the Wehrmacht on the Ostfront was forced to make hard decisions regarding the allocations of their remaining Panzer divisions. The perception in Berlin was that the Red Army would continue to concentrate their efforts from Ukraine due to past successes in this area as well as the strategic opportunities that it presented. The most likely direction of the attack was expected to be from Ukraine through Lvov into central Poland. This can be seen in the deployment pattern of the Panzer force on the Ostfront. HG Nord Ukraine was favored with about half of the Panzer force, while HG Mitte was only a fifth of overall strength. Further evidence of this can be seen in the allocation of the prized Panther and Tiger tanks where HG Nord Ukraine received about three-fifths of the total. HG Mitte had only a single Tiger battalion and no Panther tanks.

German tank and AFV strength by army group, 15 June, 1944							
	Pz. II	**Pz. III**	**Pz. IV**	**Panther**	**Tiger**	**StuG**	**Total**
HG Nord							
Operational		16	36	5	34	241	**332**
Repair	2	7	14	7	23	53	**106**
Sub-total	*2*	*23*	*50*	*12*	*57*	*294*	**438**
HG Mitte							
Operational	26	22	8		29	404	**489**
Repair	3	2	9			76	**90**
Sub-total	*29*	*24*	*17*		*29*	*480*	**579**
HG Nord-Ukraine							
Operational		75	423	175	157	480	**1,310**
Repair		33	50	17	33	70	**203**
Sub-total		*108*	*473*	*192*	*190*	*550*	**1,513**
HG Süd							
Operational		23	95	46	22	194	**380**
Repair		16	20	42	9	62	**149**
Sub-total		*39*	*115*	*88*	*31*	*256*	**529**
Russian Front							
Operational	26	136	562	226	242	1,319	**2,511**
Repair	5	58	93	66	65	261	**548**
Total	**31**	**194**	**655**	**292**	**307**	**1,580**	**3,059**

The Red Army's 1944 summer campaign began on June 9 with an attack in Karelia to knock Finland out of the war. This T-34 is a relatively old example from the 1942 production from Gorkiy Factory No. 112. These older tanks were more often seen on the Leningrad Front than elsewhere in the Red Army due to its isolation in 1942–44 during the siege of the city.

The Red Army plan for the summer offensive was based on a series of five cascading offensive surges starting from north to south. The first would take place against the Finnish army in Karelia, intending to knock Finland out of the war and end the threat to Leningrad from the north. This was a relatively small operation compared to the other offensives. The first major offensive would be Operation *Bagration*, a pincer movement aimed at encircling and destroying forward German defenses in Belarus. Operation *Bagration* was named after the Russian prince who had died in battle against Napolean at Borodino. To support *Bagration*, the third wave would be a push out of Ukraine, striking at HG Mitte's southern flank around Lvov. This would be followed by sequential strikes out of Ukraine towards central Poland around Lublin. Finally, the Red Army's southern wing would strike into Romania.

To reinforce Berlin's mistaken assessment of Soviet intentions, the Red Army began a major *maskirovka* (deception) campaign, aimed at convincing the Germans that the main blow would come against HG Nord Ukraine. The *maskirovka* campaign consisted of hiding the transfer of reinforcements to the Belorussian fronts as well as creating false troop dispositions opposite HG Nord Ukraine. The reinforcement for the Belarussian offensive consisted of moving the 5th Guards Tank Army and 28th Army from southern Ukraine, the 2nd Guards Army and 51st Army from the Crimea, and the 6th Guards Army from the Baltic.

Operation *Bagration*

On June 6, 1944, the Western Allies landed in Normandy, starting the campaign for France. This cemented a large portion of the Panzer force away from the Russian Front and so precipitated the start of the Soviet 1944 summer offensive. This began on June 10, 1944, with a local offensive north of Leningrad by the Leningrad and Karelian Fronts intended to knock Finland out of the war. The Finnish army had heavily fortified the Karelian isthmus, so the Red Army made heavy use of tank and artillery support to overcome the Finnish defenses. Soviet forces included 628 tanks and self-propelled guns, a 6:1 advantage over the Finns. The Finnish army put up a determined defense, but there was no doubt that the Red Army would eventually overwhelm them. On June 21, Finland began diplomatic steps to extricate itself from the war and a truce was arranged later in the month.

Soviet mobile formations assigned to Operation *Bagration*					
Fronts	1st Baltic	3rd Belarussian	2nd Belarussian	1st Belarussian*	Total
Tank armies		1			**1**
Tank corps	1	3		2	**6**
Mechanized Corps		1		1	**2**
Cavalry Corps		1		1	**2**
1st Belarussian Front includes only right wing assigned to Bagration					

A column from the 25th Guards Tank Brigade, 2nd Guards Tank Corps passes through the Belarussian capital, Minsk, on July 3, 1944. The T-34-85 is armed with the S-53 gun in the configuration manufactured at the Gorkiy Factory No. 112 in the spring of 1944. The GAZ-AA truck to the left is armed with a German war-booty 2cm Flak 38 automatic cannon.

On the eve of the Soviet offensive, HG Mitte had very modest Panzer resources. The 20.Panzer-Division was the only Panzer division in HG Mitte while there were four Panzergrenadier divisions (14., 18., 25., and Feldherrnhalle), equipped mainly with StuG III assault guns in their Panzer regiments. Most of the AFV strength in HG Mitte was in the separate StuG brigades and in the Panzerjäger battalions of the infantry divisions. The heaviest concentration of armor was with the 4.Armee defending Orsha which had 40 tanks including 29 Tiger Is of s.Pz.Abt.501 and 246 Stug IIIs.

The relative balance of forces in Belarus was heavily in the Red Army's favor, with the number of troops and artillery in a 3:1 ratio. In terms of tanks and AFVs, the disproportion was even more striking, with 4,000 Soviet tanks and AFVs to about 935 German vehicles, a 4:1 ratio. Hitler declared the cities of Vitebsk, Orsha, Mogilev, and Bobruisk to be *Festung* cities, meaning that they would be held to the last man. These orders limited German tactical flexibility in Belarus and assisted in the Soviet plans to envelope and destroy key German garrisons.

A column of T-34 tanks of the 1st Ukrainian Front advance during the July 1944 offensive. The lead tank is the configuration adopted in the autumn of 1943 by adding a commander's cupola to the Gayka turret to improve the commander's situational awareness.

On June 22, the Red Army began "reconnaissance in force" in Belarus. This was three years to the day from the start of the German invasion of the Soviet Union, Operation *Barbarossa*. The date was a coincidence; the start of Operation *Bagration* had been delayed by logistical considerations. The delay led to further imbalances in the tank balance after Berlin decided to reinforce the Western Front with units originally allotted to the East including Panzer-Lehr Division and the 9.Panzer-Division.

The formal start of Operation *Bagration* was at 0500hrs on June 23, 1944, beginning with a massive artillery preparation all along the front. German accounts of the artillery preparation describe it as being of an intensity and destructiveness never before seen during the war.

Soviet vs German armored dispositions at the start of Operation *Bagration*

Fronts	1st Baltic	3rd Belarussian	2nd Belarussian	1st Belarussian*	Total
Soviet Tanks & AFVs	687 (43)**	1,810 (86)	276	1,297(72)	**4,070**
German tanks & AFVs	130	316	120	366	932
Soviet/German AFV ratio	5.1:1	5.7:1	2.4:1	3.6:1	4.3:1

*1st Belarussian Front includes only right wing assigned to Bagration

**Number in parentheses is the number of Soviet engineer tanks (mine-rollers, flame-throwers)

In the north, the 1st Baltic and 3rd Belarussian Fronts enveloped the exposed German defenses in Vitebsk. Having trapped much of the 53.Armeekorps, the 6th Guards Army, spearheaded by the 1st Tank Corps, began its exploitation northwest towards Polotsk.

Much of the terrain in Belarus was not ideal for mechanized operations, especially south near the Ukrainian border due to the sodden Pripyat marsh region. Some of the best terrain was in the center, along the key Moscow–Minsk highway from Smolensk to Orsha. This area had seen bitter fighting in the autumn–winter of 1943–44, so not surprisingly the Germans had heavily fortified and mined it. The highway defenses were based around the 78.Sturm-Division, the most powerful German infantry formation in Belarus. It had unusually strong Panzer support including 31 StuG III assault guns and 18 Nashorn 88mm self-propelled anti-tank guns. Its southern flanks were covered by the 25.Panzergrenadier-Division, a relatively well-equipped force with an organic Panzer battalion equipped with StuG III assault guns.

The Soviet attack towards Minsk was conducted by the left wing of the 3rd Belarussian Front and the right wing of the 2nd Belarussian Front. The Soviet 11th Guards Army attacked down the Smolensk–Minsk corridor using special assault groups. These were composed of engineer and tank units specially configured to breach defensive belts. Each of the three assault groups consisted of a company of 10 T-34 fitted with mine-rollers, followed 150m behind by a heavy tank regiment with 21 IS-2 or KV tanks, followed 150 to 200m behind by a heavily armed assault engineer battalion, followed another 200m behind by a heavy assault gun regiment

E

T-34-85, 2ND GUARDS TANK CORPS, SUMMER 1944

The 2nd Guards Tank Corps used a white arrow symbol with a Cyrillic letter on top and a tactical number below. This insignia combination was carried on the front sides of the turret and repeated on the turret rear. The letter identified the corps' three brigades, based on the name of the brigade commander: "L" (4th GTB, Oleg A. Losik), "B" (25th GTB, Semën M. Bulgin), and "N" (26th GTB, Stepan K. Nesterov). The first digit of the three-digit tactical number indicated the brigade "1" (4th GTB), "2" (25th GTB), and "3" (26th GTB). For some unexplained reason, the tactical number on the right turret side and turret rear frequently has an "A" suffix added. For Operation *Bagration*, most of the unit's tanks had a broad white air identification stripe painted down the center of the glacis plate, over the center of the roof, and continuing over the engine deck and rear plate. This was applied in lime or some other washable paint, and so disappeared as the summer went on.

1. The top illustration shows the T-34-85 (Factory No. 112) number L 145 of the 4th Guards Tank Brigade that was commanded by Guards Junior Lieutenant D. G. Frolikov. This was one of the first Soviet tanks to enter Minsk on July 3, 1944. It carried the name "*Chervonniy*" ("Scarlet red") on the turret sides.

2. The inset drawing on the right shows a T-34-85 of the 26th Guards Tank Brigade with the tactical number N 318A.

3. The T-34-85 (Factory No. 112) at the bottom was from the 25th Guards Tank Brigade with the tactical number B 244. As can be seen, the tactical number on the left side of the turret lacks the "A" suffix that is present on the right side as shown in **4**.

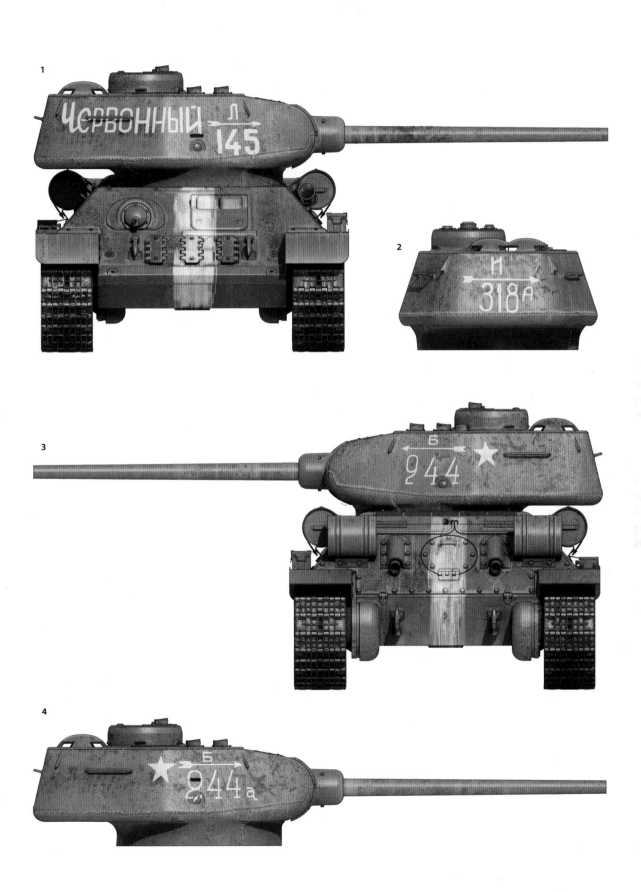

RIGHT

On August 2, 1944, Polish insurgents of the Armia Krajowa knocked out a Jagdpanzer 38 of 2./Heeres-Panzerjäger-Abteilung 743 that was passing through Warsaw on the way to the front. The vehicle was badly burned by Molotov coktails and was originally used as a road block. It was subsequently put back into running order and named *Chwat* (Daredevil). It saw some use during the Warsaw Uprising but was buried under rubble near the main post office in early September. This is a view of the vehicle after it was recovered after the war.

FAR RIGHT

At dusk on August 18, 1944, about 18 Panther tanks of 5.Kompanie and 8.Kompanie, SS-Pz.Rgt.5 "Wiking" attempted to counter-attack Soviet penetrations southwest of the Tłuszcz railway station in the direction of Jasienica. They were caught between the 2nd and 3rd Battalions of the 59th Guards Tank Brigade, taking heavy losses. The Soviet tankers claimed to have destroyed 10 Panther Ausf A tanks and captured three more that had bogged down. This photo, taken the following day, shows no fewer than seven of the Panthers.

with 21 ISU-152s. Behind all this armor and fire power came the initial wave of the rifle regiments, supported by a flamethrower tank company and a light assault gun regiment with SU-76s. As impressive as this assault appeared to be on paper, it bogged down in the strong initial defensive line. The armored support floundered on mines and tank traps, and tenacious German infantry lurked in trenches with Panzerfaust anti-tank rockets. In spite of the problems, the outskirts of Minsk were reached by July 2.

The attack by Konstantin Rokossovsky's 1st Belarussian Front in the south had the most spectacular results. Front engineers had created causeways through the Pripyat marshes in the weeks prior to the attack. This allowed the 1st Guards Tank Corps to appear unexpectedly on the southern side of Bobruisk while the 9th Tank Corps pushed past German defenses around Rogachev. HG Mitte attempted to respond using the 20.Panzer-Division, but it was unable to intervene before the Soviet pincers had crossed the Berezina river. A pocket developed near Bobruisk containing much of the 35.Armeekorps and 41.Panzerkorps totaling about 75,000 troops. A Kampfgruppe of the 12.Panzer-Division transferred from the neighboring HG Nord managed to reach the pocket and retrieve about 10,000 troops. In the meantime, fast-moving Red Army tanks bypassed the pocket and left the clean-up of the Bobruisk pocket to follow-on Soviet rifle divisions. The soggy terrain in southern Belarus led the Red Army to deploy Lt.Gen. I.A. Pliev's Cavalry-Mechanized Group, which proved to be ideally suited to the deep exploitation role. This hybrid formation consisted of the 1st Mechanized Corps and the 4th Guards Cavalry Corps. It crossed the Ptich river in late June and interdicted the Minsk-Baranovichi highway by July 2, severely compromising German defenses.

The unfolding disasters engulfing Heeresgruppe Mitte led to the relief of Generalfeldmarschall Ernst Busch on June 28 and his replacement by the commander of HG Nord-Ukraine, GFM Walter Model. Hitler regarded

F **PANZERJÄGER IN OPERATION *BAGRATION***

1. 7.5cm PaK 40/1 Marder 1 Geschützwagen Lorraine, Panzerjäger-Kompanie.256, 256. Infanterie-Division, Minsk area, July 1944. Small numbers of the old Marder 1 were still in service in the summer of 1944 in some infantry divisions' Panzerjäger companies. This vehicle is painted in the usual RAL 7028 dark yellow, with patches of RAL 6003 olive green and RAL 8017 red brown. There is a round spot on the superstructure side where a spare roadwheel had previously been carried.

2. StuG IV, unidentified unit, Heeresgruppe Mitte, Minsk area, July 1944. This Stug IV was abandoned in the Minsk area in early July 1944. It may have been stationed with one of the infantry division's Panzerjäger companies, or with one of the six StuG brigades in the area at the time. This vehicle is painted in the usual RAL 7028 dark yellow, with patches of RAL 6003 olive green and RAL 8017 red brown. The gun barrel is dark-gray heat-resistant primer.

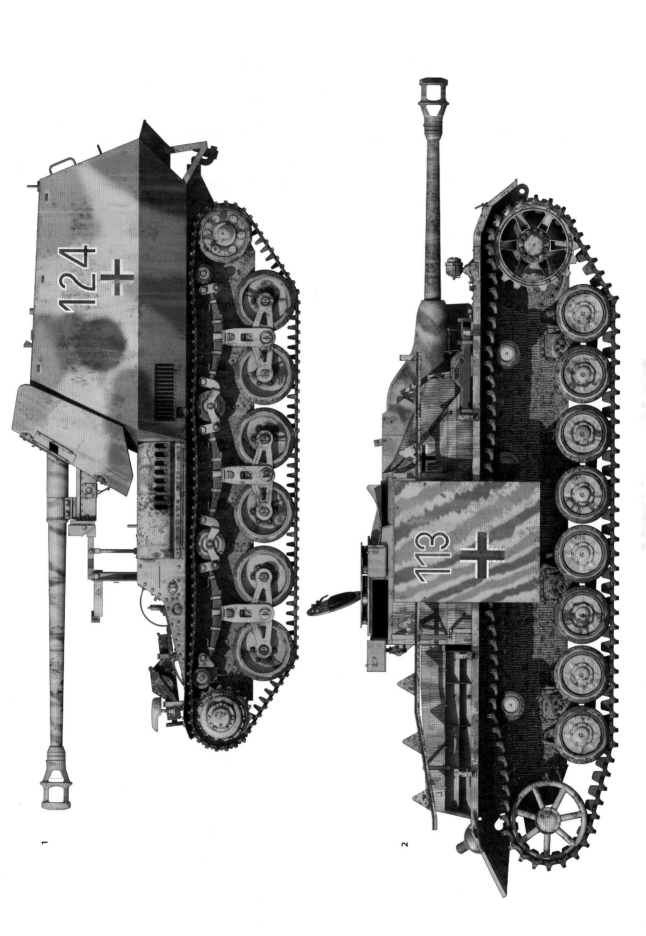

1

2

SS-Sturmbannführer Hubert-Erwin Meierdress (right), commander of I./SS-Panzer-Regiment 3, 3.SS-Panzer-Division "Totenkopf" talks to another soldier near a T-34-85 of the 3rd Tank Corps, 2nd Tank Army had knocked out in Modlin during the battles of IV.SS-Panzer-Korps near Warsaw in August 1944.

Model as his "miracle worker" and Model set about trying to transfer Panzer divisions from elsewhere on the Russian front to prop up the collapsing defenses of Heeresgruppe Mitte.

Soviet units reached the Belarussian capital of Minsk on July 2 with Pavel Rotmistrov's 5th Guards Tank Army leading the advance. The city was bypassed by most of the tanks units and liberated on July 3 against very modest German resistance. In the north, another cavalry-mechanized group consisting of the 3rd Guards Mechanized Corps and 3rd Guards Cavalry Corps began a concerted attack against the 5.Panzer-Division and 39.Panzerkorps to control the key road junction at Molodechno along the Lithuanian border. In less than two weeks since the start of the offensive, the Wehrmacht lost 25 divisions and about 300,000 men during the initial encirclement battles. According to Soviet accounts, the Wehrmacht lost 732 tanks and AFVs during the fighting from June 23 to July 7, consisting of 305 destroyed in combat and 427 abandoned.

Model won Hitler's approval for the transfer of further Panzer reserves in the hopes of redeeming the situation, with the 7.Panzer-Division entering the northern battles and the 4.Panzer-Division in the southern sector. In the meantime, the 3rd Belarussian Front reached the Lithuanian capital of Vilnius on July 8, and began systematic urban fighting against the German defenders before the city fell on July 13. A Kampfgruppe of the 6.Panzer-Division managed to penetrate 30 km into the city and recover some of the garrison before the Red Army gained full control. By mid-July, the Wehrmacht had lost a further 100,000 troops. The Red Army advance through Belarus gradually petered out by the end of July due to an exhaustion of supplies as well as significant losses of equipment and troops. Tank losses in the 5th Guards Tank Army were so high that Pavel Rotmistrov was relieved of command. Nevertheless, Heeresgruppe Mitte had been comprehensively defeated and the path opened towards Lithuania and central Poland.

The Lvov-Sandomierz Offensive

The success of the Red Army in Belarus led to the decision to continue the cascading offensives in other sectors during July 1944. The most significant of these was the Lvov-Sandomierz offensive by Ivan Konev's 1st Ukrainian Front against Heeresgruppe Nord-Ukraine. This sector had by far the strongest German Panzer concentrations at the start of the summer, but by mid-July, they had been substantially reduced due to gradual transfers to Belarus. On June 10, this sector had twelve Panzer and Panzergrenadier divisions, but by July 13, this had been reduced to only six. German/Hungarian strength in this sector was about 805 tanks and 230 self-propelled guns.

The 1st Ukrainian Front had substantial armored forces including the 1st Guards, 3rd Guards and 4th Tank Armies as well as two cavalry-mechanized groups. The front's constituent forces included seven tank corps, three mechanized corps, four separate tank brigades, 18 separate tank regiments

and 24 self-propelled artillery regiments totaling 1,578 tanks and 463 self-propelled guns. The Red Army enjoyed a roughly 2:1 advantage of tanks in this sector. This was not as great as the advantage that had prevailed in the initial *Bagration* offensive in Belarus.

The Lvov offensive was conducted along two axes. The northern thrust aimed at Rava-Russkaya toward the western side of Lvov. The southern axis was aimed directly toward Lvov. The offensive began on July 13. Soviet scout units on the northern axis found many of the German forward defense lines unoccupied and Soviet mobile units were able to move 15km westward by day's end. Due to the weakness of German defenses on the northern approaches, S.V. Sokolov's Cavalry-Mechanized Group was able to advance quickly toward Lvov, trailed by the 1st Guards Tank Army. HG Nord-Ukraine attempted to blunt this penetration by using the 16. Panzer-Division and 17.Panzer-Division, but they failed in their mission. The 16.Panzer-Division disengaged from the battle and moved to Lvov in time to take part in the defensive battle there.

German defenses in the immediate vicinity of Lvov were denser and more effective, and frustrated the advance of the 1st Ukrainian Front along the southern axis. After a difficult two days of fighting, Soviet forces finally made penetrations through the German defenses near Koltov. HG Nord-Ukraine attempted to squash the penetration using the 1.Panzer-Division and 8.Panzer-Division. The German forces were unable to hold back the Soviet tide, but progress along the southern axis was much more difficult than the drive north of Lvov. The decisive breakthrough was the advance by Sokolov's Cavalry-Mechanized Group and the 1st Guards Tank Army. By July 23, ten days after the start of the offensive, the 1st Guards Tank Army had reached deep into Poland around the old Austro-Hungarian fortress city of Przemyśl, the "Verdun of the Eastern Front" in World War I. By July 27, Sokolov's Cavalry-Mechanized Group had reached to within 20km of the Vistula river

ABOVE LEFT
T-34-85 tanks of the 53rd Guards Tank Brigade, 6th Guards Tank Corps first encountered Tiger II tanks near the village of Ogłędów, Poland, on the west bank of the Vistula river on August 12, 1944. The smiling officer near the center of this picture is Lt. Aleksandr P. Oskin, commander of the T-34-85 tank that knocked out three of the Tiger II tanks.

ABOVE RIGHT
The combat debut of the Tiger II tank on the Russian Front started inauspiciously when s.Pz.Abt.501 disembarked in Kielce with their 45 new tanks in early August 1944. They were ordered to counter-attack the Soviet bridgehead over the Vistula near Sandomierz. This Befehlspanzer command tank was one of three ambushed by a T-34-85 tank of the 53rd Guards Tank Brigade.

G

TANK SKIRMISH AT OGŁĘDÓW

On August 11, 1944, the 53rd Guards Tank Brigade sent Lt. Aleksandr Oskin's T-34-85 to the village of Ogłędów on a scouting mission. After seeing that the village was occupied by the Germans and reporting to the brigade, Oskin parked his tank in a cornfield outside the village. The crew camouflaged the vehicle using corn stalks. The following day, a column of new Tiger II tanks of s.Pz.Abt.501 headed out of the village past Oskin's camouflaged tank. The Germans were about 200m away when Oskin gave the order to fire sub-caliber (HVAP) at the tanks. In a short engagement, Oskin knocked out three of the German tanks, two of them burning out completely. One of the tanks, a Befehlspanzer command tank, was later recovered and is on display at the Russian tank museum at Kubinka.

A Tiger II of 3./s.Pz.Abt.501 and a StuG III lie abandoned after a German attack on the Soviet Vistula river bridgehead near Sandomierz was repulsed during the August 1944 fighting. In the foreground is a Soviet Maxim water-cooled machine gun.

Panzergrenadiers follow a Panther Ausf A tank, of I./Pz.Rgt.27, 19.Panzer Division during the fighting around the Magnuszew bridgehead over the Vistula in mid-August 1944.

in central Poland. Under these circumstances, HG Nord-Ukraine abandoned the defense of Lvov and attempted to redeploy westward. By July 29–30, the 1st Ukrainian Front had established small bridgeheads over the Vistula south of Warsaw. This led to a vicious series of bridgehead battles as the Wehrmacht attempted to stamp out the Soviet penetrations while the 1st Ukrainian Front made steps to reinforce the forces on the western bank of the Vistula.

Another wave of Soviet attacks began on July 18 from the southern wing of Rokossovsky's 1st Belarussian Front emanating out of the Kovel region towards the Bug river and the Polish city of Lublin. The initial attack by Soviet rifle divisions finally penetrated the German defenses along the Bug river after four days of fighting, and on July 22, the deep exploitation phase began. The 2nd Tank Army began a rapid push towards Lublin and the Vistula river while the 11th Tank Corps and 2nd Guards Cavalry Corps moved to the northwest towards Siedlice, threatening to trap embattled units of the retreating HG Mitte. On July 25, the 2nd Tank Army made a river crossing of the Vistula near Magnuszew.

In view of the disastrous situation, GFM Model was able to win Berlin's approval to rush Panzer forces into the Warsaw area to prevent the total collapse of HG Mitte. With the approach of the Red Army, the Polish Home Army (*Armia Krajowa*) staged an uprising in Warsaw, further complicating the German defenses. The poorly armed insurgents were eventually crushed after more than a month of fighting, but the uprising blocked many of the key road and rail routes for the Wehrmacht's attempts to reinforce the front.

By the first week of August, Soviet tank units were showing signs of mechanical and logistical exhaustion, and now faced a growing German counterblow. The 3rd Tank Corps was hit by the Hermann Göring Panzer Division and the 19th Panzer Division. Further Panzer units joined the fray including the 5.SS-Panzer-Division "Wiking" and the 4.Panzer-Division. The Red Army pulled the 2nd Tank Army out of the line for re-equipment, replacing it with rifle divisions to take up a defensive posture east of Warsaw. Stalin had no enthusiasm to assist the Polish insurgents in Warsaw, but in mid-September he permitted a modest river-crossing attempt by the 1st Polish Army from the Praga suburbs which lasted about a week before being forced back over the Vistula on September 23.

By the end of September, there was a stalemate along the Vistula river front as both sides licked their wounds. Moscow was undoubtedly pleased by the exceptional success of the *Bagration* offensive, and rather than risk creating a narrow salient towards Berlin, decided to exploit the German difficulties on either flank for their political opportunities.

The Iaşi-Chişinău Offensive

By September 1944, the Red Army offensive operations into Poland came to a halt and switched to a defensive posture. By this stage, Soviet mechanized formations had endured significant losses and were mechanically exhausted. These sectors would remain largely static until the Vistula–Oder Offensive of January 1945. Instead, the Red Army shifted its focus to its northern and southern flanks.

The southern attack was conducted by the 2nd and 3rd Ukrainian Fronts against Heeresgruppe Süd. The strategic objective was to knock Romania and Bulgaria out of the war, capture Germany's main fuel supply at the Romanian Ploesti oil fields, and open a secondary route to Berlin via Budapest and Vienna from south of the Carpathian Mountains. HG Süd had only about 170 Panzers and assault guns, and about half of its troops were from the Romanian army. The two Soviet Fronts had a modest superiority in the number of troops, and were supported by 1,874 tanks and AFVs, a ten-fold advantage against the German and Romanian forces.

An SU-85 tank destroyer with tactical number S-13 of the 1443rd Self-propelled Artillery Regiment, 23rd Tank Corps, 2nd Ukrainian Front, passes through Bacău, Romania, on August 24, 1944. The street is lined with Romanian soldiers since, the day before, the king had declared that Romania was abandoning the alliance with Germany.

The Iaşi-Chişinău (Iassy-Kishniev) offensive began on August 20 with the 2nd Ukrainian Front trying to secure bridgeheads over the Prut river near Iaşi while the 3rd Ukrainian Front pushed out of a small bridgehead over the Dnestr river. The Romanian troops showed no enthusiasm to continue the war on Germany's side, and on August 23, the pro-German government in Bucharest was overthrown. Romania's defection ensured a collapse of HG Süd-Ukraine and the best that could be accomplished was a rearguard delaying action to withdraw as many troops as possible. The German 6.Armee was trapped in a pocket near Chişinău and conducted a costly retreat to the Siret river where its remnants were trapped and destroyed by September 5. German units in Romania were routed and lost about half their men and most of their equipment. The Romanian army switched sides, and was thrown into action against their erstwhile German allies during the advance towards Hungary.

A column of Lend-Lease M4A2 medium tanks of the 6th Tank Army pass through a Romanian city in August 1944. This is from the later 1943 production series with the enlarged driver hatches.

BATTLE ANALYSIS

Through the summer of 1943, the Germans had been able to maintain a combat equilibrium on the Russian Front by offsetting their numerical weakness with technological advantages, as well as superior crew and small unit

A war-booty StuG III Ausf G assault gun serving with the 5th Guards Tank Brigade of the 4th Ukrainian Front in September 1944. At the time, the brigade had two StuG III assault guns and a Tiger tank. It has the slogan *"Smert' nemetskim okkupantam!"* ("Death to the German Occupiers") painted on the front plate.

performance. In 1943, the Red Army lost four Soviet tanks for every German tank lost, thereby dulling the impact of Soviet numerical advantages. However, by 1944 the Germans were not able to maintain this equilibrium due to the revival in Soviet tank design, substantial Panzer transfers to Western Europe in the spring of 1944 to deal with the forthcoming Allied invasion of France, and a diminishing disparity in German vs Soviet tactical skills. From a broader perspective, German operational skills were hampered by Hitler's "do-or-die" rigidity. Conversely, the Red Army was displaying new-found operational skills, learned at a bitter cost after three years of war.

Comprehensive tank loss statistics for the summer 1944 campaign on the Russian Front are not available, although some data is available. Soviet data is available for certain campaigns and for certain major formations, but not for the entire campaign or all units. There is German data from the quartermaster of the Generalinspekteur der Panzertruppe, but this data is evidently incomplete. As can be seen on the accompanying chart, see overleaf, this is most obvious in the case of certain discrete categories, for example the line for the Tiger II which lists no losses although Tiger II losses obviously occurred. As described in more detail in a companion volume in this series, this data also suffers from a very murky definition of losses where some combat losses were not written off until months after the battles when it became evident that damaged vehicles kept on inventory

A pair of Panther Ausf A tanks of 4./Panzer-Rgt. Großdeutschland on August 7, 1944, near Vilkaviškis, Lithuania, close to the East Prussian frontier.

were not repairable and the losses were irrevocable.[1] From the available data, the disparity in Soviet vs German AFV losses was not as dramatically different as it was in 1941–43.

Soviet tank and AFV losses in the 1944 summer campaigns[2]

Campaign	Total losses	Avg. daily loss
Karelian Offensive in Finland, 10 Jun–9 Aug	294	5
Operation Bagration, 23 Jun–29 Aug	2,857	43
Lvov-Sandomierz Offensive, 13 Jul–29 Aug	1,269	26
Iași-Chișinău Offensive, 20–29 Aug	75	7.5
Total	**4,495**	

German AFV losses in the East: summer 1944

	Jun	Jul	Aug	Sep	Total
PzKpfw II	0	65	5	15	*85*
PzKpfw III	0	0	0	8	*8*
PzBefWg/Beo III	1	39	14	0	*54*
PzKpfw 38(t)	0	0	0	2	*2*
PzKpfw IV	10	256	309	134	*709*
Panther	17	241	246	136	*640*
Tiger I	11	166	76	57	*310*
Tiger II	0	0	0	0	*0*
Panzer sub-total	39	767	650	352	*1,808*
StuG III	79	887	293	321	*1,580*
Sturmpz IV	0	5	0	2	*7*
StuG Sub-total	79	892	293	353	*1,617*
Marder I	2	6	0	1	*9*
Marder II	2	49	7	7	*65*
Marder III	11	264	44	67	*386*
Nashorn	36	34	7	32	*109*
PzJg Sub-total	51	353	58	172	*634*
Total	**169**	**2,012**	**1,001**	**877**	*4,059*

Data from OKH, Heeres-Waffenamt

1   Steven Zaloga, *German Tanks in Normandy 1944*, Osprey New Vanguard 298, 2021.
2   Krivosheyev, G. F. (ed.), *Rossiya i SSSR v voynakh XX veka: Kniga poter* (Veche, Moscow: 2010), pp. 520–21.

During the course of the summer's fighting, Heeregruppe Nord was pushed down the Baltic coast from the Leningrad area to the Kurland peninsula near Riga in Latvia. Among the units trapped there was the 4.Panzer-Division. This is a PzKpfw IV Ausf H. of 6./Panzer-Regiment.35 defending a trench line on the Kurland peninsula in the early autumn of 1944. The unit's distinctive bear insignia can be seen on the turret's armor skirts.

The Soviet data tends to go into more detail about the source of losses. The accompanying chart lists Red Army tank and AFV losses by gunfire versus mines/obstacles and enemy aircraft. As is evident from comparing the Soviet data to German claims, the Luftwaffe claims were particularly exaggerated. This is far from unique; Allied aircraft claims of the destruction of Germans tanks in Normandy were also very inflated.

Soviet tank and AFV losses in guards tank armies, 1944 summer campaigns					
	Starting strength	Gunfire losses*	Mine losses	Aviation losses	Total losses
1st Gds Tank Army					
Lvov 15 Jul–20 Aug					
T-34	430	638 (95%)	4 (1%)	28 (4%)	670**
Other tanks + SU	194	214 (82%)	5 (2%)	37 (14%)	261
All tanks + SU total	624	852 (92%)	9 (1%)	65 (7%)	926
2nd Gds Tank Army					
Lublin Aug 1944					
T-34	473	492 (92%)	14 (3%)	29 (5%)	535
Other tanks + SU	337	234 (92%)	8 (3%)	13 (5%)	255
All tanks + SU total	**810**	**726 (92%)**	**22 (3%)**	**42 (5%)**	**790**
3rd Gds Tank Army					
Lvov 14 Jul–31 Aug					
T-34	510	454 (87%)	23 (4%)	46 (9%)	523
Other tanks + SU	101	213 (81%)	6 (2%)	52 (19%)	262
All tanks + SU total	**611**	**667 (85%)**	**29 (4%)**	**98 (11%)**	**785**
5th Gds Tank Army					
Minsk 23 Jun–20 Jul					
T-34	314	218 (86%)	14 (6%)	22 (9%)	254
Other tanks + SU	202	122 (88%)	15 (11%)	2 (1%)	139
All tanks + SU total	**516**	**340 (87%)**	**29 (7%)**	**24 (6%)**	**393**

*Includes anti-tank rockets

**Total losses sometimes exceed starting strength due to reinforcement of the tank armies during the campaign

The chart here shows the German assessment of Soviet tank/AFV losses in the summer of 1944 based on claims by the Heer/Waffen-SS/Luftwaffe ground forces and Luftwaffe aviation units. The German *Fremde Heere Ost* (Foreign Armies East) intelligence agency collated these claims and then applied a deflator to the totals based on previous estimates of exaggerated kill claims. Aircraft kill claims were deflated more sharply than those from ground units. Even if the German claims were not especially accurate, they do provide a guide for the intensity of the summer battles.

German kill claims against Soviet tanks and AFVs 1944					
Claims	Jun	Jul	Aug	Sep	Total
Army	838	3,875	4,373	2,339	11,425
Luftwaffe	46	417	257	135	855
Subtotal	**884**	**4,292**	**4,630**	**2,474**	**12,280**
Adjusted*					
Army	590	1,940	2,190	1,640	6,360
Luftwaffe	20	210	130	70	430
Total	**610**	**2,150**	**2,320**	**1,710**	**6,790**

*Estimated claims after adjustment by Fremde Heere Ost intelligence agency

FURTHER READING

Adair, Paul, *Hitler's Greatest Defeat: The Collapse of Army Group Centre, June 1944*, Arms & Armour, London (1994)

Bączyk, Norbert, *Warsaw II: The Tank Battle at Praga July–September 1944*, Leandoer & Ekholm, Stockholm (2009)

Dunn, Walter, *Soviet Blitzkrieg: The Battle for White Russia 1944*, Stackpole, Mechanicsburg (2008)

Glantz, David and Orenstein, H. (eds), *Belorussia 1944: The Soviet General Staff Study*, Frank Cass, London (2001)

Glantz, David and Orenstein, H. (eds), *The Battle for Lvov 1944: The Soviet General Staff Study*, Frank Cass, London (2002)

Harrison, Richard (ed.), *The Iasi-Kishinev Operation: The Red Army's Summer Offensive into the Balkans*, Helion, Solihull (2022)

Harrison, Richard (ed.), *Operation Bagration: The Rout of the German Forces in Belorussia-Soviet General Staff Study*, Helion, Solihull (2016)

Kozitsyn, Vyacheslav, *Ostfront Panzers: Belorussia 1943–44*, Kozitsyn, Nizhni-Tagil (2021)

Krivosheyev, G. F. (ed.), *Rossiya i SSSR v voynakh XX veka: Kniga poter*, Veche, Moscow (2010)

Müller-Hillebrand, Hermann Burkardt, *Der Zweifrontkrieg: Das Heer vom Beginn des Feldzuges die Sowjetunion bis zum Kriegsende, Band III*, E. S. Mittler & Sohn, Frankfurt (1969)

Magnuski, Janusz, *Wozy Bojowe LWP 1943-1983*, WMON, Warsaw (1985)

Nash, Douglas, *From the Realm of a Dying Sun. Volume I: IV. SS-Panzerkorps and the Battles for Warsaw July-November 1944*, Casemate, Havertown (2019)

Nebolsin, Igor, *Pervaya iz gvardeyskikh 1-ya gv. Tankovaya armiya v boyu*, Yauza, Moscow (2016)

Nebolsin, Igor, *Stalin's Favorite: The Combat History of the 2nd Guards Tank Army from Kursk to Berlin, Vol. 2*, Helion, Solihull (2015)

Nebolsin, Igor, *Tank Battles in East Prussia and Poland 1944–1945*, Helion, Solihull (2019)

Niepold, Gerd, *Battle for White Russia: The Destruction of Army Group Centre, June 1944*, Brassey's, London (1987)

Shirokorad, A. B, *Tankovaya voyna na vostochnom fronte*, Veche, Moscow (2009)

Shein, Dmitriy, *Tanki vedet Rybalko: Boevoy put 3-y gv. tankovvoy armii*, Yauza, Moscow (2007)

Zaloga, Steven, *Bagration 1944: The Destruction of Army Group Centre*, Osprey Campaign 42, Osprey (1996)

Zaloga, Steven and Ness, Leland, *Red Army Handbook 1939–1945*, Sutton, Stroud (1998)

n.a., *Boevoy sostav sovetskoy armii, jan.-dek., 1944 g.*, Voenizdat, Moscow (1990)

This is one of three Panther Ausf A tanks of SS.Pz.Rgt.5, 5.SS-Panzer-Division "Wiking," captured by the 59th Guards Tank Brigade, 8th Guards Tank Corps on August 18, 1944 in the area between Jasienica and Tłuszcz after they became bogged down during the fighting. The Soviet tankers recovered the tanks and they were subsequently deployed by the corps' 62nd Guards Heavy Tank Regiment.

INDEX

Page numbers in **bold** refer to illustrations and their captions.